CHICAGO BEER

 A History of Brewing, Public Drinking and the Corner Bar

JUNE SKINNER SAWYERS

AMERICAN PALATE

Published by American Palate
A Division of The History Press
Charleston, SC
www.historypress.com

Copyright © 2022 by June Skinner Sawyers
All rights reserved

First published 2022

Manufactured in the United States

ISBN 9781467149259

Library of Congress Control Number: 2021952403

Notice: The information in this book is true and complete to the best of our knowledge. It is offered without guarantee on the part of the author or The History Press. The author and The History Press disclaim all liability in connection with the use of this book.

All rights reserved. No part of this book may be reproduced or transmitted in any form whatsoever without prior written permission from the publisher except in the case of brief quotations embodied in critical articles and reviews.

I am drinking ale today.
—Edgar Allan Poe

Hallelujah, I'm over joyed
I'm drunk again and I'm unemployed.
—Michael McDermott, "Unemployed"

Ain't nothin' that a beer can't fix
Ain't no pain it can't wash away.
—Thomas Rhett, "Beer Can't Fix"

CONTENTS

Cheers 7
Introduction 11

1. Saloons and Breweries on the Midwestern Prairie:
    From the Sauganash Hotel to Tied Houses 13
2. Hinky Dink, Bathhouse John and the Rise and Fall
    of the Vice District 31
3. Temperance, Prohibition and Organized Crime 53
4. The Craft Beer Revival: Goose Island and Beyond 75
5. Community in a Glass: The Corner Bar 93

Resources 119
A Subjective List of Classic Chicago Bars 121
Notes 127
Bibliography 137
About the Author 144

CHEERS

Chicago Beer got its start as a guide to craft breweries in Chicago for indie publishers Deirdre Greene and Nigel Quinney. It has since morphed into the current project. Either way, whether one says cheers, prost, sláinte, na zdrowie, skol or salud, thanks are in order. With that in mind, I would like to offer my gratitude to the brewers, craft beer owners and other like-minded folk who took the time to answer my queries. They include the following: Jeff Marshall at Heartland Beer, Phil Williamson-Link at Pipeworks, Keith Peltz and Todd Rudolf at Two Brothers, J.P. Glunz, Adam Cieslak, Elonzo L. King III at Maplewood, Eric Hobbs at Solemn Oath, Jennifer Galdes at Grapevine PR, Zoe King at On Tour, Aila Myers and Brian Pawola at Pollyanna, Jay Cassel at Short Fuse, Brian Buckman at Illuminated Brew Works, Jason Vucic at Sidelot, Thomas Creech at Goose Island, Dan Schnarr at Lagunitas, Donn Bichsel Jr. and John Carruthers at Revolution, John Freyer at Argus, Matthew Modica at 5 Rabbit, James Owen at 3 Sheeps, Sean Mahoney at BuckleDown, Amy Jones at Burnt City, Hagen Dost at Dovetail, Katy Tilley and Matt Potts at Destihl, Kaitlyn at Begyle, Flavio Gentile and Mason Sane at Printers Row Wine Shop, Andrew Burns at Emmett Brewing, Neil Byers at Horse Thief, Pat Buckstaff at Lake Shore Beverage, Cesar Marron at Sketchbook, Wesley Phillips and Bob Iggins at Windy City Distributing, Bill Hurley at Empirical, Charlie and Katie Davis at Right Bee Cider, Tommy Vasilakis at Brickstone, Lisa Gregor at Church Street, Michael Carroll and Brian Schnell at Band of Bohemia, Josh Gilbert at Temperance, Gary Gulley at Alarmist, Brad

Cheers

Zeller at Aleman, Eileen Fitzgerald at Corridor, Sara Taylor and Meredith Anderson at Half Acre, Beau Forbes at Goose Island, Martin Coad and Michael Cameron at Greenstar/Uncommon Ground, Ben Ustick at Off Color, Trevor Rose-Hamblin at Old Irving Brewery, Jason Klein at Spiteful, Tom Piekarz and Ed Marszewski at Marz, Jared Rouben and Jeremy Cohn at Moody Tongue, Brian Taylor at Whiner, Catherine Price at Ravinia, Bruce Dir at Tighthead, Mike Condon at Noon Whistle, Tom Korder at Penrose, Amy Kamp at Evil Horse, Josh Mowry at Miskatonic, Jake Guidry at Hopewell, Karl Rutherford at Twisted Hippo and Jeremiah Zimmer at Hop Butcher for the World.

Sandy Vox, when she was the assistant sales manager for Total Alcohol Beverage at Jewel Osco, introduced me to many of the above-named brewers, and for that I am forever grateful. Theresa Nugent, Cheryl Sauter, Linda Odegard, Ann Dobbyn, Megan Emish and Tim Gunderson accompanied me on my research and made what was already fun even more enjoyable. During one busy Christmas season, I spent a pleasant afternoon talking to Katala, the bartender at the Field Museum Bistro, whose knowledge of the collection of Field beers was impressive, and several equally pleasant afternoons with Charles Troy in the northern suburbs.

I am indebted to the work of the many fine journalists and historians who have chronicled and continue to chronicle the history of beer and brewing in Chicago, especially Rich Lindberg, Dave Hoekstra (Dave's blog is a marvel) and the king of Chicago saloon culture, Bill Savage. Thanks to Paul Durica for introducing me to the work of Kathleen Judge. (Thanks, Kathleen, for allowing me to use your wonderful Beer Lager Riot poster.) And thank you also to Warren Leming for sharing his knowledge about Nelson Algren and beer culture in general.

Josh Noel's vast knowledge of beer, and the culture of beer, is impressive; it's always a pleasure reading his work in the *Chicago Tribune*. Thanks to Liz Garibay for her efforts at the Brewmuseum, as well as the entertaining and informative beer seminar at the Newberry Library that I attended on a Saturday afternoon in July with co-presenter Brian Alberts. Erica Gunderson of WTTW's *Chicago Tonight* was kind enough to share her Hinky Dink recipe. Thanks to Ben Gibson and Hilary Parrish at The History Press for their expertise and feedback along the way. It's been fun.

Theresa Albini and I spent several sun-soaked weeks visiting breweries in Illinois, Indiana, Wisconsin and Michigan. Research! She also took some wonderful photographs for the book.

CHEERS

Finally, cheers to my local, Kasey's Tavern in Printers Row, and their great staff, including Kelsey Kellgren and Shelby Williams. Here's to the new friends I met there: Lisa Browne, Matt Fiedler, Alfred Thomas and Adam Navarro.

INTRODUCTION

The origin of breweries and drinking establishments in Chicago dates back to its earliest days on the Illinois prairie when the indomitable saloonkeeper and fiddler Mark Beaubien opened the Hotel Sauganash in 1831.

Drinking in the Windy City has deep roots.

Beer scholar Liz Garibay fights the perception that "alcohol dumbs down history." On the contrary, she insists that liquor, and beer in particular, is a "driving cultural force."

Indeed, the history of beer and saloon culture has been the subject of countless books, articles, classes and, a few years ago, even a conference. On October 24–27, 2019, the Smithsonian Institution in partnership with the Brewseum, a nonprofit organization dedicated to telling the global story of beer, held a conference on beer and culture at various sites in Chicago, including the Field Museum and Metropolitan Brewing.

Chicago Beer explores the origins of drinking and brewing in Chicago and the growth of brewing as an industry, from the earliest days to the temperance movement and Prohibition to the glory days of the tied houses and up to the current craft beer revival.

In addition, *Chicago Beer* explores the cultural significance of the corner bar—a neighborhood staple—and how it fits into the larger context of the social fabric, as well as confronting the devastating effect of the pandemic

Introduction

on the brewing industry. Corner bars, notes *Chicago Tribune* beer writer Josh Noel, "are vehicles to the past." Finally, it features numerous sidebars, including brief portraits of historic saloonkeepers, profiles of historic Chicago bars and even a discussion of the art of the beer label (many beer labels acknowledge their historic roots or historic figures in Chicago history).

Chapter 1
SALOONS AND BREWERIES ON THE MIDWESTERN PRAIRIE

From the Sauganash Hotel to Tied Houses

I keep the tavern like Hell, and I play the fiddle like the Devil.
—attributed to Mark Beaubien

By all accounts, Mark Beaubien knew how to throw a party. He was an ebullient presence in the little frontier town of Chicago. Outgoing, a born raconteur—and a fine fiddler to boot—Beaubien could even be called Chicago's first saloonkeeper. He was certainly the most famous and the most beloved.

Beaubien was the younger brother of Fort Dearborn trader Jean Baptiste Beaubien. With his wife, Monique, and their six children (he would have twenty-three!), he arrived in Chicago from Detroit in 1826 at the advice of his older sibling. The Beaubiens bought a small cabin on Wolf Point from James Kinzie, son of early settler John Kinzie, considered Chicago's first permanent white settler, and traded with the Indigenous Native American population.[1] (Years later, Wolf Point, the location where the north, south and main branches of the Chicago River came together, would be the inspiration for the Y-shaped symbol that can be seen on many public buildings in Chicago.) Within a few years, the Beaubiens began to accept guests at their little cabin, which they initially called the Eagle Exchange Tavern. Beaubien would later change the name to the Sauganash Hotel, which, like many prairie establishments, was also a tavern; thus, the Sauganash Hotel was the first saloon in Chicago.

Wolf Point in 1832. The birthplace of Chicago and Chicago saloonkeeping. *Author collection.*

THE EARLIEST DRINKING ESTABLISHMENTS were rudely constructed inns erected with just the barest of materials. They had names like the Wolf Tavern or the Green Tree Tavern (more about that later) and typically served whiskey and brandy and various victuals, while offering a place to rest one's weary head.

Unlike in eastern cities, public taverns evolved differently in midwestern towns like Chicago. During the early decades, most retail liquor sales were made not in inns or taverns but more likely in general stores and groceries, according to historian Perry Duis. Wholesalers opened "sample rooms" where customers could purchase alcohol on a wholesale basis while sampling the goods before they bought anything. Eventually, these early inns were replaced by higher-quality hotels so that by the late 1850s, the word "saloon" began to be used rather than tavern or inn, the latter of which referred "to a retail establishment" that sold liquor.[2]

IN JUNE 1830, MARK Beaubien acquired a license to operate a tavern within the confines of his hotel, which at the time was still called the Eagle Exchange. He moved the business to the southeast corner of Market Street (now North Wacker Drive) and Lake Street and gave the new structure a new name, the Sauganash Hotel, in honor of his friend Billy Caldwell, whose Indian name was Sauganash. Caldwell was an Indian interpreter who was also half Native American: his father was an officer in the British army stationed in Detroit; his mother was Potawatomi. Sauganash means the equivalent of "Englishman" in the Potawatomi language.

At the time Beaubien opened the Sauganash, the tiny settlement consisted of only a dozen or so houses. The place that Beaubien had settled in was barely a village, let alone a town. But there was something about it—its location at the mouth of a river on the edge of a great lake that resembled an ocean—that appealed to him. It was a primitive place by modern standards. But it was also a place to start over, to begin again. And with the jaunty Beaubien as host, word soon spread far and wide as not only the hotel became famous but also Beaubien himself.

The Sauganash was described as a white two-story building with bright blue shutters. It appealed to settlers and Natives alike. The tavern was attached to the hotel at what is now the corner of Wacker and Lake, a stone's throw from the river. It was a lively place if you didn't mind roughing it a bit. Guests slept on the floor while Beaubien, ever the enterprising entrepreneur, was said to rent blankets for fifty cents a night.

Beaubien was a gracious host. He knew how to entertain and was a wizard on the fiddle (he never referred to his instrument as a violin). He had men and women, young and old, dancing to his reels. Folks danced long into the night. Some danced *and* gambled.

One of Beaubien's favorite tunes was "The Devil's Dream," an old fiddle tune that is popular to this day (it appears in the opening scenes of Steve McQueen's acclaimed 2013 film *12 Years a Slave*). Other favorites of Beaubien's were the Scots reel "Monymusk" and the traditional Irish air "Believe Me, If All Those Endearing Young Charms," which the Irish poet Thomas Moore later set to lyrics.

John Dean Caton, a lawyer who arrived in Chicago from upstate New York in 1833 and later became chief justice of the Illinois Supreme Court, was an admirer of Beaubien's fiddling. "He played it in such a way as to set every heel and toe in the room in active motion," he wrote in his memoirs. "He would lift the sluggard from his seat, and set him whirling over the floor like mad!" He then favorably compared Beaubien's style to the great Norwegian fiddler Ole Bull. "If his playing was less artistic than Ole Bull, it was a thousand times more inspiring to those who are not educated to a full appreciation of what would now create a furore in Chicago; but I would venture the assertion that Mark's old fiddle would bring ten young men and women to their feet, and send them through the mazes of the dance, while they would sit quietly through Ole Bull's best performances."[3]

But not everyone was taken with Beaubien or his tavern on the prairie. An English traveler, Charles Latrobe, for example, described the Sauganash as a "vile, two-story barrack" filled with the "the most appalling confusion, filth and racket."

Beaubien owned the hotel until 1834. But the Sauganash was famous for other reasons. The building also was home to Chicago's first theater. Ultimately, it was destroyed by fire in 1851 and torn down. Nearly a decade

Chicago Beer

Left: Sauganash Tavern owner Mark Beaubien's fiddle. *Photo by author. Right*: Mark Beaubien, tavern owner and fiddler extraordinaire. *Author collection.*

later, the Wigwam was erected on the same site for the Republican National Convention where Abraham Lincoln was nominated on May 18, 1860. Alas, the Wigwam was also destroyed by fire, in 1867.

The site of the Sauganash Hotel and the Wigwam was dedicated as an official Chicago landmark in 2002 and rededicated on November 6, 2017. Plaques honoring the buildings are situated on opposite sides of a five-foot stone marker on the pedestrian median on North Wacker Drive near Lake Street.

In 1840, Beaubien moved to Lisle, located in DuPage County nearly twenty-five miles west of Chicago. He acquired a building originally constructed in the 1830s by William Sweet on Southwest Plank Road, now Ogden Avenue, and continued to do what he did best: entertain. He bought farmland and a cabin from Sweet and opened a saloon, the Beaubien Tavern, and then later turned it into a tollhouse—he collected tolls in front of his inn—for the Southwest Plank Road running from Lisle

A History of Brewing, Public Drinking and the Corner Bar

Sauganash Hotel plaque. Located at the southeast corner of Lake Street and Wacker Drive, the plaque commemorates Mark Beaubien's historic hotel and tavern. *Photo by author.*

to Chicago. It served as a tollhouse from 1851 to 1857. Eventually, the building was moved to Lisle Station Park as part of a museum site. It is now part of the Museums at Lisle Station Park at 921 School Street in Lisle, located a few blocks south of its original location.

Beaubien died in 1881 in Kankakee, Illinois.

Beaubien and Sauganash are commemorated in numerous ways today. There is a Northwest Side neighborhood called Sauganash, bounded by Devon Avenue on the north, the Edens Expressway on the west, Bryn Mawr Avenue on the south and the Sauganash Trail on the east. There is also a golf course, the Billy Caldwell Golf Course, and Caldwell Woods Forest Preserve. Caldwell Avenue is named after him, as is Sauganash Avenue. What's more, a short-lived brewery bore the Sauganash name and released more than a half dozen beers, many with a historic Chicago theme, including Indian Summer, Billy Caldwell IPA, Great Fire Rye PA, Corruption Porter and Wolf Point Kolsch.[4] Beaubien also has a street named after him: Beaubien Court in the Loop, Chicago's downtown.

ANOTHER PROMINENT, AND POPULAR, tavern in early Chicago was the Green Tree Tavern, built in 1833 by James Kinzie at the northeastern corner of Canal and Lake Streets. Over the years, it went through various owners and name changes and even locations before moving to its final location, in 1880, at the corner of Milwaukee Avenue and Fulton Street.

Much has been written about the Green Tree's rustic ambiance. Its bar was used not only for drinks but also for umbrellas, overcoats, whips and other nineteenth-century accoutrements. At one end of the bar were tallow candles. A tinder box was used for lighting pipes. Newspapers were available for patrons to read. Because it also served as a guesthouse, or makeshift hotel, as was typical of the era, cloth and leather slippers hung in a row

The Green Tree Tavern was another early Chicago saloon. *Author collection.*

against a wall for guests to wear at night so that mud and other dirt weren't tracked into the living area.

In the middle of the room was a large stove that was used during the cold winter months not only for obvious warmth but also for hot water to make toddies, as well as more practical functions such as shaving and washing. The dining room consisted of two room-length tables covered with a green-checkered cloth. Dinner fare might feature such dishes as wild duck, prairie chickens or wild pigeon potpie. In its later incarnations, the Green Tree became a hotel under different names and changed ownership numerous times. At one point, Abraham Lincoln reportedly was a guest when he was still a young Illinois lawyer.

In the late nineteenth and early twentieth centuries, bars sold mostly beer and whiskey. Whiskey was usually consumed straight or with a chaser, usually water or even, as strange as it sounds today, milk. These early taverns also sold nonalcoholic items such as cigars, cigarettes and chocolates.

A History of Brewing, Public Drinking and the Corner Bar

Early Brewers

In 1833, William Haas and Andrew Sulzer (also known as Konrad Sulzer) established the city's first brewery, producing English-style ales and porters. Their first-year production consisted of six hundred barrels in a town of only two hundred souls.

Three years later, in 1836, Sulzer sold his interest to William B. Ogden. Ogden built a large structure at the corner of Chicago Avenue and Pine Street (now Michigan Avenue), all while he was acting as Chicago's first mayor. Two years later, another changeover took place when William Lill, an English immigrant, bought out Haas. Lill, in turn, sold his interest to Michael Diversey.[5] In 1841, Diversey bought an interest from Ogden. Lill & Diversey Brewery was a shining success and, according to historian A.T. Andreas, "the most extensive establishment of its kind in the West." By 1861, it had grown to take over two full city blocks.

Michael Diversey served two terms as a Chicago alderman. He was also a philanthropist in the German American community and heavily involved in the Catholic Church. He donated land for the McCormick Theological Seminary and was a founder of St. Joseph Catholic Church and also donated a small plot of land where St. Michael's Church in Old Town stands today.

When Diversey died in 1869, Lill continued to operate the brewery until the Great Chicago Fire of 1871, when the brewery burned to the ground. It never reopened. Lill died a few years later in 1875.

In 2012, Warrenville-based Two Brothers collaborated with the French craft brewery Brasserie Castelain to release a dry-hopped biere de garde with notes of citrus, grass and apricot. In 2017, Goose Island's Fulton and Wood Series released Lill Moxie, a dry-hopped cream ale inspired by and paying homage to Lill and Diversey and their flagship cream ale. According to the Goose Island website: "In the days before Prohibition, Cream Ale was the preferred beer style of the blue collar worker. This clean and refreshing ale has a slightly sweet malt body and undertones of corn that complement our signature house yeast flavor." A release party took place at Manny's Deli in the South Loop on March 23, 2017.

Another early brewer was German immigrant John A. Huck. In 1847, Huck opened the first lager beer brewery in Chicago, which was bounded by Chicago Avenue and Superior Street and Rush and Cass (now Wabash Avenue) Streets. In 1855, it moved to the corner of Banks and State Streets.

Huck Brewery was one of the early German breweries in Chicago and the first brewery to feature a beer garden. *Author collection.*

Beer historian Bob Skilnik has called it "the first true lager beer brewery in Chicago." Huck brewed a malted product made from a new strain of yeast imported from Germany. This new strain, notes Skilnik, stayed fresh longer and had a pleasant and lighter taste than the heavier ales and stouts that dominated the market at the time. In fact, adds Skilnik, Huck's product was the precursor of the type of beer most Chicagoans enjoy today.[6]

Huck not only introduced Chicago to lager, a light and crisp beer that had lower alcohol content, but he also opened the first beer garden, which was attached to his brewery. The beer garden presented music, dancing, food and, of course, beer. (See chapter 3 for a discussion of beer gardens.)

STILL ANOTHER EARLY GERMAN brewer was Conrad Seipp. Seipp was born in Hessen, near Frankfort-on-the-Main, Germany. A carpenter and joiner, he immigrated to the United States in 1849, settling first in Rochester, New York, before moving to Chicago. In 1854, he opened his brewery. When it burned down, he built a second brewery at 27th Street and Cottage Grove Avenue.

Seipp started with half a dozen employees. Two years later, in 1858, he partnered with Frederick Lehman and changed the name to Seipp & Lehman. Under the new name, business flourished. After Lehman died in 1872, a year after the Great Fire, Seipp changed the name again to the Conrad Seipp Brewing Co., which became one of the largest and most successful breweries in the United States. It was the largest brewery in Chicago from 1854 to 1933. By the mid-1870s, Seipp was producing over 250,000 barrels a year. His brewery was innovative in numerous ways, including new techniques in refrigeration. He was also one of the only early brewers to export beer outside the city.

Seipp died in 1890, but family members, including his son William Conrad Seipp, continued to run the brewery even as the company merged with several smaller breweries to become the City of Chicago Consolidated

Brewing & Malting Co. Grain shortages during World War I and the arrival of Prohibition devastated the beer industry overall. The company survived, but barely, by producing "near beer" and distributing soft drinks. Seipp shut down operations altogether in 1933 as the Prohibition era was coming to an end. The building was demolished to make room for Michael Reese Hospital.

In 2020, Laurin Mack, Seipp's great-great-great-granddaughter, resurrected the brand with Pre-Prohibition Lager, using a recipe from the Seipp vaults. A subsequent release, Columbia Bock, in March 2021 was originally brewed for the 1893 World's Columbian Exposition. A limited release, Mack worked in collaboration with Metropolitan Brewing on the North Side to produce this Columbia Bock. She also partnered with Metropolitan to bottle and brew Seipp's Extra Pale, crafted in the "pre-Prohibition pilsner" style and brewed with traditional North American malted barley, corn and Bohemian and Heritage hops.

STILL ANOTHER PROMINENT BREWER was Peter Schoenhofen, a Prussian immigrant who worked in the brewing industry. In 1861, he partnered with Martin Gottfried and opened a brewery at Canalport and 18th Street in the Pilsen neighborhood. Several years later, in 1867, Schoenhofen bought out Gottfried and became the Peter Schoenhofen Brewing Co. During the 1890s, the company was owned by the London-based City Contract Co., but by the turn of the century, the Schoenhofen family had regained control under the name of the National Brewing Co. It was under this name that the company sold its popular Edelweiss brand. Seventeen buildings once occupied the site. Now only two buildings remain: the administration building, constructed in 1886, and the powerhouse, erected in 1902. The area is known as the Schoenhofen Brewery Historic District.

Schoenhofen shut down during Prohibition but reopened after the failed experiment ended. In the late 1940s, the Atlas Brewing Co. purchased it. Later, in the early 1950s, it became part of Drewery's Ltd. based in South Bend, Indiana.

Other early breweries included Wacker & Birk Brewing and Malting Co. at 171 North Desplaines Street, McAvoy Brewery on 24th Street and South Park Way (now Martin Luther King Jr. Drive) and F.J. Dewes Brewery Co. at the corner of Hoyne and Rice.

The Growth of the Brewing Industry

Beer production grew quickly during the first few decades of Chicago's existence. By the turn of the nineteenth century, the city by the lake had more than fifty breweries, mostly run by German immigrants. The growth of the industry led to competition among brewers.

The completion of the Chicago & North Western Railway in 1857 allowed Milwaukee brewers to ship beer to Chicago, and the widespread adoption of pasteurization made it possible to transport cold beer hundreds of miles away without fear of spoilage.

The 1871 Great Chicago Fire was devastating on so many levels, killing approximately 300 people and leaving more than 100,000 people homeless, with much of the central business district destroyed. It also decimated the fledgling brewing industry, including Lill & Diversey and John Huck's brewery. Neighboring Milwaukee, Wisconsin, sent water and beer to the parched residents. In particular, the Milwaukee-based Schlitz sent beer to the ravaged city by train, ostensibly as a goodwill gesture, but it also made good business sense. This generous act of kindness earned the brewer a loyal and grateful customer base and led to its popular ad slogan: "The beer that made Milwaukee famous."[7]

Almost 400,000 barrels of beer were brewed in Chicago a few years after the fire, in 1879. By 1890, Chicago had more than thirty breweries. Immigrants of German descent (74 percent of all Chicago brewers in 1900, according to the Landmark Commission), as well as immigrants from England and Canada, dominated the brewing industry. In addition to Huck, Schoenhofen and Seipp, some of the other German brewers were Joseph Theurer, Francis Dewes and Michael Brand. The popularity of German brewers and German-run saloons led Chicagoans to turn away from heavier ales to the lighter and more effervescent lagers.

During the early days of the brewing industry, beer was sold in draft, but by the 1850s, more and more beers were sold in bottles. Popular demand for beer led to a supply problem: too much demand and not enough breweries to fill the demand. Unable to make beer fast enough to meet market demands, cities like St. Louis and especially Milwaukee brought their beer through the newly built railroads. By 1855, there were 675 saloons in Chicago, the vast majority owned by German and Irish immigrants. From the 1860s to the 1870s, lager became more popular than English-style beers. By the late nineteenth century, lager dominated the entire brewing industry in the United States. Much of its popularity was fueled by waves of immigrants from Germany, Ireland, Bohemia and Scandinavia.

The Science of Brewing

Technological advancements in brewing took place in Chicago during the early decades of its history. The Siebel Institute of Technology, the oldest and longest-running brewing school in the United States, was an especially important institution.

John Siebel was born near Dusseldorf, Germany, in 1845. He moved to Chicago in 1866 with a PhD in physics and chemistry from the University of Berlin. In his adopted city, he became chief chemist at a sugar refinery and also worked as a chemist for Cook County before partnering with fellow German brewer Michael Brand. They established a scientific school for brewers in 1882. Although unsuccessful, Siebel tried again, in 1890, opening the Zymotechnic Institute. In 1910, the name was changed to the Siebel Institute of Technology, a vocational college offering technical courses in both English and German on brewing, malting, fermentation and bottling that offered entry-level, intermediate-level and advanced-level courses in brewing. Siebel also for a time edited the trade magazine the *Western Brewer*. Founded in 1876, it was the longest continually published brewing journal in the industry until it ceased publication in 1960.

During most of its history, Siebel was family owned until 1992, when it was sold to Quest. In 2000, it was sold to the yeast manufacturer Lallemand in Montreal. In early 2020, the Siebel Institute of Technology moved from its Kendall College location on Goose Island to 322 South Green Street in the Greektown neighborhood.

The Know Nothings Start a Riot

To say that Chicago has had a complex relationship with saloons and the consumption of alcohol is an understatement. As early as 1833, Chicago had a local chapter of the American Temperance Society (ATS), which was founded in Boston in 1826.

The temperance movement was a social movement created partly by women who advocated against the consumption of alcoholic beverages. In particular, the movement was fueled by a desire to protect women and children from the troubling effects of men's alcohol abuse. Supporters took a pledge to abstain from drinking distilled beverages (although wine and beer were allowed, as was the medicinal use of alcohol). The temperance movement was also part of a larger nineteenth-century reform sentiment that included the abolitionist movement and women's suffrage movement. Followers of the movement, sometimes referred to as "drys," condemned saloon culture and the public disorder that they thought it encouraged. One specific goal of the drys was to force saloons to close in the evening and on Sundays. Over the years, political pressure mounted until the Illinois legislature passed a Sunday closing law in 1851 even though, in Chicago at least, it was widely ignored.

But when Levi Boone, a distant relative of Daniel Boone, was elected mayor in 1854, things changed. Boone was supported by members of the Know Nothing Party, which consisted of a coalition of drys, anti-immigrant voters and native-born Americans largely of Protestant faith and English ancestry who were alarmed by the huge waves of Catholic, largely Irish immigrants, immigrating to the United States in the 1840s and 1850s, especially after the Great Irish Famine of 1847. Boone also happened to be a teetotaler with an intense dislike of beer, which he viewed as un-American. In his mind, "real" Americans drank whiskey, not beer brewed by the "foreign" element (roughly half of Chicago at the time was foreign born, and of those immigrants, half were Germans who had an indisputable fondness for beer).

In response, Boone raised the annual saloon license fee from $50 to an astounding $300 and demanded that the city enforce the state's Sunday closing laws. Numerous saloonkeepers objected and, in defiance, kept their saloons open, denouncing it as being the most tyrannical and undemocratic measure since the Stamp Act during the Revolutionary War. Ultimately, more than thirty saloon owners were arrested for violation of the law. They were scheduled to appear in court before Judge Henry Rucker on April 21, 1855. On the day of the trial, protesters gathered outside the old Cook County Courthouse, clashing with police. One person died, and dozens were arrested. The episode came to be known as the Lager Beer Riot. Beer historian Liz Garibay has called the riot the "first moment of social unrest in Chicago."[8]

For many German and Irish immigrants, the Sunday closing laws were seen as an affront to their culture. Brewers and saloon owners also opposed the law for obvious reasons: their livelihoods were at stake. The following year, voters booted Boone out of office, and his reforms were reversed.

But the drys didn't give up. They turned their attention to the so-called high license movement. Ostensibly, the intent behind the movement was to increase the annual saloon license fee in order to raise revenue for social programs caused or aggravated by the abuse of alcohol. The higher fees were also an attempt to force saloons out of business. It took a while, but by

1883, Illinois passed the Harper High License Act, which raised the annual saloon license fee from $103 to $500. The law had an immediate and stinging effect: nearly 800 of the 3,500 saloons in Chicago closed.

Saloonkeepers were in dire straits. With nowhere else to turn, they asked brewers for assistance in paying the exorbitantly high license fees. Brewers didn't want the saloons to close since they would lose a major source of their own revenue, so they agreed to subsidize the owners by paying part or all of the fees, with the caveat that the saloonkeeper would exclusively sell the brewer's beer. This tit for tat arrangement meant that more than five hundred new saloons were able to open the following year because of the subsidies from breweries. This measure also led to a system known as tied houses.

Tied Houses

A tied house was a type of saloon that had its origins in the United Kingdom, especially in England. The tied house system had a profound impact on pre-Prohibition Chicago. In England, commercial breweries consolidated retail outlets by purchasing or controlling pubs; tied houses referred to taverns owned by breweries. In other words, the tied houses sold only beer made by the breweries that owned them.

The tied system in Chicago began in 1892 when English syndicates the Chicago Brewing & Malting Company and the Milwaukee & Chicago Breweries Ltd. bought saloons as well as land with the idea of building new ones. The most prolific of the tied house builders was the Milwaukee-based Joseph Schlitz Brewing Company. But Schlitz wasn't the only brewer that built tied houses in Chicago. Other Milwaukee brewers also built them, including Pabst, Miller and Blatz. Local brewers also built their own tied houses, including Atlas, Birk Brothers, Gottfried, Peter Hand, Standard and Stege.[9]

The tied house system emerged in Chicago during the late nineteenth and early twentieth centuries because of three major reasons: 1) competition among breweries, 2) legal restrictions and 3) social pressures on public drinking establishments. If a saloonkeeper agreed to serve only one brand of beer, he got a lot in return. The brewer provided cash and loans as well as equipment and even paid the license fee, which could be expensive. The tied house system also brought its share of advantages to brewers: it guaranteed retail outlets for their beer; it allowed brewers to control how their beer was stored; and it maintained a brand's reputation for quality. In essence, it was a form of quality control.

As Perry Duis has noted in his book *The Saloon: Public Drinking in Chicago and Boston, 1880–1920*, the tied house system transformed saloonkeepers from entrepreneurs to employees. Daniel Okrent called tied houses "subsidized servants of the institutions that paid for everything: the breweries themselves."[10] The proliferation of saloons was an ironic and unexpected consequence of the tied house system. Tied houses were found along major thoroughfares but also on quiet residential streets. By 1891, there were 5,600 saloons in Chicago.[11]

Specifically, the tied house system referred to direct control of saloons by large brewing companies that sold their beer exclusively in their saloons. Breweries purchased existing saloons, and later, they erected their own tied house buildings. According to the Landmark Designation Report, at least forty-one tied house buildings survive in Chicago. Milwaukee brewers, including Schlitz, Peter Hand, Standard and Stege, built most of the tied houses.

In addition, brewers thought the tied system would improve the image of the saloon. As we will see in the next chapter, the pre-Prohibition saloon was denounced for its wickedness and dissolute patrons. Brewers rented commercial property that sold only their products and hired their own employees, similar to today's franchise system. Critics decried tied house breweries as soulless giant monopolies. The proliferation of tied houses was one of the contributing factors that, ironically, led to Prohibition: during the 1890s, the number of saloons in Chicago increased dramatically, which led to intense competition and price wars among breweries. There were so many saloons on the city streets that it inevitably led to a backlash as temperance and other anti-alcohol reformers denounced the negative effects that booze had on the citizenry.

The tied house system ended with the arrival of Prohibition in 1919. Tied house buildings that reopened as saloons after the repeal of Prohibition were owned or leased by independent tavern owners.

Tied House Architecture

Tied houses were important for another reason: their architecture. The architectural design of tied houses tended to be well crafted, distinctive and even respectable. Because of their high quality, they contributed positively

A History of Brewing, Public Drinking and the Corner Bar

Schlitz Brewery tied house plaque. The former tied house was built in 1903 by the architectural firm of Frohmann (also spelled Frommann) & Jebsen. The building houses Schubas Tavern, a live music venue. The club's restaurant is appropriately named Tied House. *Photo by author.*

to the character of Chicago neighborhoods even as the reason for their existence—they were saloons, after all—was often looked down upon. The architectural firm of Frohmann & Jebsen designed many of the tied houses, usually in a German Renaissance, Queen Anne or Baroque style.

Milwaukee's Schlitz Brewing Company was the most prolific builder of tied houses. During the tied house era, Schlitz purchased saloons in Chicago where it could exclusively sell its products. Schlitz owned not only the saloon but also the equipment, even down to the glassware and signage. The saloonkeepers paid for the beer and leased the equipment. At the time, Schlitz was the third-largest brewer in the United States, after Pabst and Anheuser-Busch. Under the management of Edward G. Uihlein, Schlitz built fifty-seven tied houses from 1897 to 1905, mostly on corners of commercial streets in working-class ethnic neighborhoods. Schlitz houses were renowned for their distinctive features, such as a belted globe with a red-and-cream brick color scheme.

The Schlitz company has a rich backstory. In 1848, entrepreneur August Krug emigrated from Germany to Milwaukee, where he opened the Little Germany restaurant and tavern. His small batches of lager were so popular among his largely German clientele that he opened his own brewery, the August Krug Brewery, in the basement of the establishment. In 1850, Krug hired another German émigré, Joseph Schlitz, as bookkeeper. When Krug died in 1856, Schlitz took over and in 1858 changed the name to the Joseph Schlitz Brewing Company.

In 1872, Edward Uihlein was hired to become the manager of the expanding Chicago market. (Years earlier, in 1850, Krug had adopted his eight-year-old German nephew August Uihlein; Edward was one of August's brothers.) Schlitz brewed in Milwaukee and shipped it to the Chicago plant, which was located near the Chicago & North Western Rail tracks at Ohio and Union Streets. Tragically, three years later, in 1875, Joseph Schlitz and more than three hundred people died in a shipwreck off the Isles of Scilly, some twenty-six miles west of the Cornish peninsula, while returning from Germany. His body was never found.

Schlitz Row

In 1904, Schlitz Brewery bought a ten-acre plot of land across the Illinois Central Railroad tracks at 115th Street outside Pullman. Pullman was a planned community founded by industrialist George Pullman. Pullman revolutionized train travel with the invention of the Pullman sleeping car, which allowed passengers to endure uncomfortable and, often, interminable rail journeys. But he was a practical businessman at heart. In 1880, he founded the utopian company town of Pullman on the western shore of Lake Calumet so that his employees could work and live in a safe and peaceful environment, far removed from the corruption and vice of the city.

Most of the residential units consisted of row houses as well as apartments and single-family homes. The town had its own newspaper, church, schools and hospital. The Arcade consisted of a theater, a library, a post office, a YMCA, a bank and shops. Annexed to Chicago in 1889, Pullman hired Dutch, Swedish, German, English and Irish workers.[12] Although the Pullman Company employed African Americans as porters, they were not allowed to actually live in Pullman.

Pullman was hardly a worker's paradise. George Pullman expected and demanded that workers abide by his high standards. During hard times, he reduced hours and slashed wages while maintaining the same level of rent. As one Pullman resident said, "We are born in a Pullman house, taught in the Pullman school, catechized in the Pullman church, and when we die we shall be buried in the Pullman cemetery and go to the Pullman hell."

And Pullman was dry.

Taking advantage of an opportunity when he saw it, Edward Uihlein erected a two-block string of saloons, stables and apartments that earned the moniker of Schlitz Row not in Pullman itself but just outside its boundaries.

Schlitz Tied Houses

More than forty tied houses still remain in Chicago. Here are some significant examples:

- 1393–99 West Lake Street in the Fulton Market district. Former home of La Luce restaurant.
- Schubas Tavern, 3159 North Southport Avenue (1903; Frohmann & Jebsen). German Renaissance Revival. Features multicolored brickwork, bonnet roof and the distinctive Schlitz logo with its belted globe.*
- Southport Lanes & Billiards, 3325 North Southport Avenue. Ornate murals depict wood nymphs in a Germanic forest. In September 2020, it shut down only to reopen in 2021 (thanks to a $70,000 state grant)—and then sadly, in July 2021, shut down again—permanently.
- 2159 West Belmont Avenue (1903–4; Charles Thisslew). Queen Anne style. It is now a Starbucks.
- 3456 South Western Avenue (1899; Kley & Lang). Queen Anne style.
- 958 West 69th Street (1898). Queen Anne style.
- 11400 South Front Avenue (1906; Frohmann & Jebsen). Queen Anne style. In the Roseland neighborhood.
- 11314 South Front Avenue (1906; Frohmann & Jebsen). Schlitz Brewery stable building. Queen Anne style.

In June 2020, the Commission on Chicago Landmarks recommended landmark status for the former Schlitz tied house at 9401 South Ewing Avenue on the far South Side. The building also had an eight-room former boardinghouse in the rear. Scenes from the 2020 FX television show *Fargo* were shot at the bar. As of this writing, owners Mike Medina and Laura Coffey Medina plan to open a new tavern, the East Side Tap, in 2022.

---

* The Schlitz belted globe trademark is based on sculptor Richard Bock's design for the Schlitz exhibit at the 1893 World's Columbian Exposition. Bock's original design was extravagantly imaginative: the globe was held up by four female figures representing the four hemispheres, gnomes at their feet, flanked by four pedestals made of beer kegs and, on top of each, a herald blowing a trumpet.

Schlitz Row was an ingenious idea to attract the "thirsty" workers of the town since the adjacent Roseland neighborhood was separated from Pullman by railroad tracks.

Uihlein commissioned Chicago architects Frohmann & Jebsen, Kley & Lang and Charles Thisslew to design the Schlitz tied house buildings. The structures were uniformly of high quality and distinguished and distinctive architecture. Schlitz Row was a two-block-long stretch that originally consisted of three tied houses, housing for Schlitz workers and brewery managers and a company stable for the Schlitz delivery horses. The tied house at 11400 South Front Avenue and the stable at 11314 South Front Avenue are all that remain of Schlitz Row. Argus Brewery, which closed during the COVID-19 pandemic, was located at the latter address.[13]

Previously, the architecture of the independent saloon was modest at best, often referred to as a "store and flat" building with retail space at ground level and private dwellings on the second or third floors. The tied-house system elevated the status of the buildings "to attract customers and to promote the brewer's brand."[14] Typically, the tied house buildings were located at the corners of busy commercial streets. They were highly visible. Some floors were used as meeting rooms, and some had rooms set aside for workers.

We will return to the temperance movement, including the rise of the Woman's Christian Temperance Union (WCTU), when we talk about Prohibition in chapter 3, but first let's make a detour through the vice district.

Chapter 2

HINKY DINK, BATHHOUSE JOHN AND THE RISE AND FALL OF THE VICE DISTRICT

Chicago ain't no sissy town.
—Michael "Hinky Dink" Kenna

It's a lallapalooza!
—Michael "Hinky Dink" Kenna, referring to the success of the inaugural (1896) First Ward Ball

In Chicago, politicians and saloonkeepers were natural bedfellows. Many of the most colorful—and, admittedly, corrupt—politicians in Chicago either owned saloons or were bartenders (or both). Some of the more prominent include Michael C. McDonald, Big Jim O'Leary, John Brennan, Barney Grogan, John Powers, Edward "Foxy" Cullerton, Paddy Bauler and especially the political powerhouse duo of Michael "Hinky Dink" Kenna and John "Bathhouse John" Coughlin. "Seven out of thirty-six aldermen in 1886 were saloonkeepers," asserts Perry Duis.

Grogan's West Side saloon was a hangout for pickpockets, prostitutes and gamblers. Cullerton, a descendant of one of the city's original settlers, was an alderman for nearly fifty years. His longevity had a lot to do with the favors and bribes he handed out. He was elected alderman of the Seventh Ward before the fire and served well into the 1890s. His nickname was due to his ability to produce more votes than legitimate voters.

John Brennan of the Eighteenth Ward on the West Side ran a saloon next to a police precinct station. He also had a job as a bail bondsman, which earned him more than a few votes when he became alderman. In addition, he also "provided food and lodging in exchange for voters at each year's elections."[15] He gave food to the hungry and prevented people from being evicted.

Overall, bribes and ballots went hand in hand—along with the occasional brawl. "Prior to 1886," notes Duis, "voting booths appeared in the back rooms of saloons and sometimes in front of the bar. This put the appropriate bribe of a free drink only an arm's length away."[16]

The intersection of saloons and politicking has been around for a long time, but it had to begin somewhere.

Michael Cassius McDonald was considered Chicago's first crime "boss." A born hustler and the so-called king of the gamblers, in 1884 McDonald opened a combination gaming parlor/saloon called the Store at the corner of Clark and Monroe. The gambling area was located on the second floor, in between a legitimate liquor business on the street level and McDonald's private quarters on the third floor. Every game was fixed, although that apparently didn't detract much from its popularity, which led McDonald—not, as common consensus has it, P.T. Barnum—to utter the immortal line, "Don't worry, there's a sucker born every minute."

While at the height of his reign, "King Mike" controlled the ward committeemen, aldermen, mayors, senators and governors, wielding the kind of power not seen again until the rise of Al Capone. If you wanted anything done, you went to Mike. The entire police department was said to be under his wings. He made his fortune through gambling profits, protection money and a bookmaking syndicate. But he also supplied a service. He would obtain bail bonds, fix juries, pay off authorities and deliver votes for his "customers."[17]

After McDonald's death in 1907, a new gambling king emerged on the scene: Big Jim O'Leary. O'Leary was a gambling man with the magic touch and a reputation as a "square shooter." When, during the "Fight of the Century" in 1892, the whole word seemed to bet on John L. Sullivan, O'Leary, ever the contrarian, chose "Gentleman" Jim Corbett.

And won.

O'Leary was born at 137 DeKoven Street, the son of Patrick and Catherine O'Leary (yes, his mother was the famous Mrs. O'Leary of the now-debunked the cow-kicked-over-the-lantern fame). After the fire and the subsequent shame associated with it, the family moved to the nearby Back of the Yards neighborhood.

As a teenager, O'Leary began working for bookies at the famous Union Stock Yards. By the early 1890s, he had opened his own saloon at 4183

> ### "Chicago Ain't Ready for Reform"
>
> Arguably, Paddy Bauler was the last saloonkeeper-alderman. He is best remembered today, if he is remembered at all, as once saying, "Chicago ain't ready for reform," uttered after Richard J. Daley won the 1955 mayoral election over incumbent Martin Kennelly.* During Prohibition, he ran a speakeasy at Willow and Howe in Lincoln Park. When the noble experiment ended, he opened a saloon at 403 West North Avenue, which, in the great tradition of Hinky Dink Kenna, also served as his ward office. And also like Hinky Dink—and Bathhouse John Coughlin—he controlled gambling and vice in his ward.
>
> Bauler had another trait in common with Coughlin: he also liked to wear flamboyant clothing. Although not as garish as Bathhouse, Bauler was known to don on election night at least a high silk hat while downing a stein or two of beer and typically singing "Chicago, That Toddlin' Town."
>
> Son of a German immigrant, Bauler's actual first name was Matthias, but he adopted the Irish moniker of "Paddy" for political reasons, figuring that having an Irish first name couldn't hurt as a Chicago saloonkeeper/politician.
>
> He was alderman of the Forty-Third Ward from 1933 to 1967.
>
> ---
>
> *Is that what he actually said? According to Edward McClelland, the actual quote was the less colorful, "Chicago ain't ready for a reform mayor." A different version of the quote—"Chicago isn't ready for reform yet"—appeared in the February 24, 1955 edition of the *Chicago Tribune*.

South Halsted Street in the same neighborhood. It was no ordinary saloon. It featured Turkish baths, a restaurant, a billiard room and a bowling alley. It also had secret rooms. His perfectly legal saloon was separated from the next-door building, where illegal operations took place, by internal double iron doors. Among its features were trapdoors, a fake chimney with a ladder leading to the basement and a poker room and bookie parlor in the rear. Steel doors on stairs from the poker room on the second floor led to a vacant room on the third floor, with the pool hall and bookie parlor in the rear. O'Leary bet on everything, no matter how big or how small.

O'Leary died at 726 West Garfield Boulevard from natural causes in early 1925.

If McDonald and O'Leary earned their respective titles as the gambling kings of Chicago, the self-proclaimed "Negro Gambling King" was John "Mushmouth" Johnson, the most famous Black vice lord of his day. Johnson worked as a waiter at the Palmer House, where he made invaluable contacts with the city's movers and shakers before opening his own saloon and gambling den, the Emporium Saloon, in 1890. Located along the heart of Whiskey Row, a shadow land of cheap saloons that lined the west side of State Street south of Van Buren and a mere stone's throw from Mickey Finn's notorious Lone Star Saloon (for more about Finn, see below), the three-story structure offered billiards on the first floor, craps and roulette on the second and poker on the third. Johnson collected protection money from the gambling and opium dens in Chinatown then located on South Clark Street. Living up to his reputation as a loyal lieutenant, he reliably delivered the Black vote to First Ward aldermen Kenna and Coughlin. Lloyd Wendt and Herman Kogan even went so far as to call Johnson a "close friend" of Hinky Dink.[18]

Johnson was also something of a philanthropist, giving generously to the Black community. What's more, he had several surprising family and work-related connections: his sister, Dora, was married to Jesse Binga, Chicago's leading Black businessman and banker. His nephew was the poet Fenton Johnson (in 2016, Fenton was inducted into the Chicago Literary Hall of Fame). And former colleague Robert Motts owned the Pekin Theatre at 27th and State Street, a famous South Side live music venue. Motts used the money he made working for Johnson to open the iconic theater. Finally, Johnson's brother Elijah opened the Dreamland Café, a South Side cabaret where the likes of Louis Armstrong, King Oliver and Alberta Hunter performed.

Hinky Dink and Bathhouse John: Lords of the Levee

They were opposites in every possible way, but despite their differences, they were inseparable in life and in work. Today, we know them by their memorable nicknames, Hinky Dink and Bathhouse John, names as intertwined in the public consciousness as Butch Cassidy and the Sundance Kid, Thelma and Louise and Frodo and Sam. Michael "Hinky Dink" Kenna and John "Bathhouse John" Coughlin were co-aldermen of the First Ward. The First Ward was not only the richest ward in the city; it was also the most corrupt. It included the

Levee, Chicago's notorious red-light district. Known by the colorful moniker "Lords of the Levee," to use Lloyd Wendt and Herman Kogan's famous phrase, they ran their ward as if it was their own private fiefdom. "Coughlin was all sound and fury; Kenna was silence and action."[19] Kenna was the brain behind the operations. Coughlin had the gift of the gab.

It was a winning combination.

BOTH MEN GREW UP among similar circumstances in an Irish neighborhood called Conley's Patch, then located around Monroe and Wells. Kenna got his famous nickname from Joseph Medill, editor of the *Chicago Tribune*, because of his short stature (he was all of five feet, one inch tall).

At the tender age of ten, Kenna left school and began selling newspapers. When he was just twelve, he borrowed money from a barkeep and purchased his own newsstand at the corner of Monroe and Dearborn. Young Kenna was a newspaper hawker, a "newsie," to use the vernacular, when he met Medill.

"What's your name, boy?" asked Medill. "Kenna's my name," the young lad replied. "That's a good Irish name," said Medill, "but I'm going to call

Michael "Hinky Dink" Kenna (*left*) and a dapper John "Bathhouse John" Coughlin (*right*), the Lords of the Levee. *Author collection.*

you Hinky Dink because you are such a little fellow." (Wendt and Kogan described him as being "a midget of a boy with an old man's face.") It's a great story but perhaps an apocryphal tale since Kenna himself denied it.

Kenna had modest ambitions. He didn't aspire to be president of the United States. All he wanted was to control the little corner of the world that he knew most intimately. He was elected alderman of the First Ward in 1897 and teamed up with his fellow First Ward alderman John Coughlin, who had been elected in 1892. Kenna held that position until 1923, when he became ward committeeman. With Coughlin, he controlled the Levee. Essentially, both men ran a protection racket; the brothels and gambling dens paid the protection money. Kenna, in particular, established an elaborate system, a defense fund, as he called it, in which a percentage of the protection money paid by madams and gamblers and the like was pooled for the hangers-on and their followers who somehow got into trouble with the law. The idea was that hoodlums partial to Kenna and Coughlin would have legal counsel provided them. It made for a perfect world where politics and crime came together in the most serpentine and interconnected fashion.

In 1897, the same year that Kenna became the co-alderman of the First Ward, Carter Harrison Jr. was elected mayor of Chicago, conveniently and partially due to Kenna's impressive organizational skills bringing in the vote. Kenna's fame grew not only throughout Chicago but across the country—indeed, throughout the world.

KENNA'S POLITICAL PARTNER IN crime, John Coughlin, learned his trade from the best—the best of the king bosses, that is. Under the tutelage of Mike McDonald, Coughlin became active in First Ward politics and eventually became president of the ward organization. He did what he was told. So when the ward bosses were looking for someone to run for alderman, they had their man.

Coughlin opened his own saloon, the Silver Dollar, at 169 East Madison Street in July 1895. He had always wanted his own saloon. But it couldn't be just any saloon. It had to be special. Coughlin commissioned a local artist to paint large silver dollars on the ceiling and walls. It was patronized by gamblers and "racing men," thieves and prostitutes.

Kenna, too, was a tavern owner. As a young boy, he ran errands for saloonkeepers, so he knew the ins and outs of the saloon trade before he opened his own saloon called the Workingmen's Exchange at 427 South

The former location of Hinky Dink Kenna's Workingmen's Exchange saloon in the old vice district, located a short walk from Printers Row. The building houses a pawnshop and a men-only hotel. *Photo by author.*

Clark Street. At eighty-four feet long, it was reportedly the longest bar in the world at the time. Another room had a lunch counter where bowls of soup were served with plenty of bread to sop it up. Beer cost five cents. Two or three times a day, Kenna came in (he had another, more respectable saloon a short walk away), emptied the contents of the drawers and placed the dough in a large sack, which he kept in a safe.

Kenna consistently violated the law by opening early and closing late. He served bums and tramps, hobos and the just plain hungry. A nickel would get you a glass of beer, "the largest and coolest in the city." Above the tavern was the Alaska Hotel, a flophouse that could accommodate as many as 250 to 300 men. Beds were rented by the week for one dollar, "and during elections twice that number."[20] "I am going to give these poor 'hobos' the best home they ever had in their lives," said Kenna.

Kenna's tavern lived up to its name: he handed out meals in exchange for votes. On Election Day, Kenna and his team rounded up the hobos and homeless in the ward, took them to the polls "and gave them marked ballots to drop in the box and bring back unmarked ballots" in return for a dollar and/or a free lunch. "The unmarked ballots were then marked again and brought to a different polling place."[21] If a customer bought a drink, the

---

THE FREE LUNCH

The origins of the free lunch predate Michael Kenna. A barkeep by the name of Joseph Chesterfield Mackin reportedly introduced the idea after his other attempts to drum up business failed. In order to attract customers, he began serving a hot oyster that came free with every drink. Most of the time, the free lunch was simple, such as cold cuts, boiled eggs or cheese with crackers.

Sometimes the lunch was not quite free—but it was a good deal nevertheless. At Kenna's Workingmen's Exchange, for example, customers could get a pair of huge pork chops, fried potatoes, four slices of toast and Hinky Dink's twenty-four-ounce schooners—all for a dime.

Otherwise, a typical free lunch might consist of crackers, cheese and "the cheaper cuts of pork and beef." It fed families and the unemployed and was a nice change of pace from the cramped tenement quarters. The back room was used for special occasions such as weddings. It was also a place to play card games and have a "serious discussions of politics."*

---

* Duis, "Saloon in a Changing Chicago," 219–20.

lunch was free and typically consisted of pickled vegetables, hard-boiled eggs and cold-cut sandwiches.

The tavern was also where Kenna gathered with his friends and business associates, where he talked the talk of politics and the street, where he "distributed happiness to the poor and unfortunate." His saloon had a national and international reputation. It was the place to see. Rudyard Kipling made a visit, as did Lincoln Steffens and H.G. Wells. Wells, in particular, took a liking to Hinky Dink himself, calling him "a straight man, the sort of man one likes and trusts at sight.…He is very kind to all his crowd. He helps them when they are in trouble, even if it is trouble with the police."[22] He helped them find work. He offered the safety net that society did not provide, extending a sympathetic ear.

In 1923, the number of aldermen per ward was reduced from two to one, while the number of wards increased from thirty-five to fifty, as it still is today. After the change, Kenna stepped down in favor of Coughlin, although he remained as the ward's committeeman. He was fine with the "demotion"—he always preferred to run things behind the scenes anyway: Coughlin had always been the public face of the First Ward democratic machine.

As mentioned earlier, after the change, the men took turns as alderman of the First Ward until Coughlin's death in 1938 at the age of seventy-eight at Mercy Hospital. Kenna retired to his quarters in the Auditorium Hotel, and when that closed, he moved to the Blackstone Hotel, where he passed away. To avoid any threat of factionalism, Kenna became First Ward alderman, taking Coughlin's place. Kenna was elected unopposed to fill his seat. But by this time he was more of a figurehead than anything else.

Red-Light Districts

Chicago had several red-light districts, or levees, over the decades. The earliest crime-ridden area dated back to the 1850s and was known as the Sands, just north of the Chicago River. Here were shanties and hovels, gambling dens, brothels and saloons, where prostitutes, gamblers and thieves thrived and where robberies were rampant and murders commonplace. Chicago had earned a reputation as a center of crime and corruption. Indeed, Chicago's vice districts were as rough-and-tumble as the gold rush boomtowns out west.

After the Great Fire, the vice district began moving farther and farther south. Before 1890, it was located in an area known as the Custom House

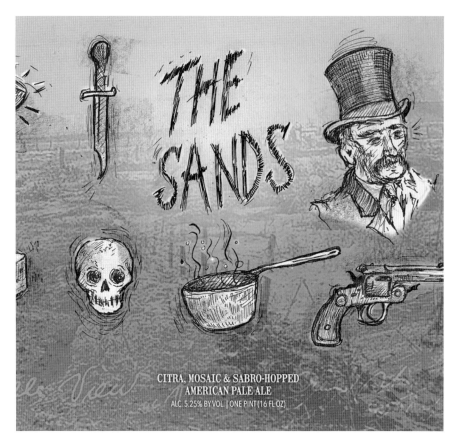

Hop Butcher for the World's the Sands citra, mosaic and sabro–hopped American Pale Ale. Dan Grzeca's suitably haunting poster features the top-hatted gentleman "Cap" Streeter, for whom the upscale Streeterville neighborhood is named. *Courtesy of Hop Butcher for the World.*

Place Levee (now Federal Street) on Plymouth Court, along State and Wabash and south to Van Buren and along Harrison and Polk in what is now Printers Row. This area was lined with brothels and saloons. Custom House Place also happened to be conveniently located down the street from Dearborn Street Station, also called Polk Street Station, where most of the travel arriving from St. Louis and other cities stopped.

But the most famous and notorious of the Chicago red-light districts was the Levee on the South Side. The Levee emerged around the time of the World's Columbian Exposition in 1893, the world so vividly depicted in Erik Larson's page-turner of a novel, *The Devil in the White City*. This South Side Levee continued for thirty or so years.

The First Ward's Levee District has been compared to New York's Tenderloin, San Francisco's Barbary Coast and New Orleans's Storyville.

The First Ward was the city's richest ward and also the most notorious since the red-light district, the Levee, was located within its boundaries. Clark Street, Wabash Avenue, 18th and 22nd Streets bound the Levee proper. As the Levee moved farther south, so did the boundaries of the First Ward.

"Along the streets jutting west from Michigan Avenue whore houses lined the cobblestones and pimps and…streetwalkers plied their ancient trades," write Wendt and Kogan. "From Cullerton Street to Twenty-second along Dearborn Avenue was brothel after brothel, duplicating in detail the notorious stretch that thirty years before had ranged along Customs House Place from Polk to Harrison Streets."[23]

The Levee was home to saloons, gambling dens, brothels, peep shows, burlesque houses, dive bars, pool halls, flophouses, chop suey joints, opium dens and tattoo parlors, as well as dice and faro houses, dime museums, concert halls and bucket shops. Off Dearborn Street were sordid little corners with evocative names like Gamblers' Alley, the Hairtrigger Block and the House of Nations.

Between the Great Fire and 1903, the Levee was considered not only the largest but also the most depraved red-light district in Chicago. Among its innovations were the so-called panel houses, which referred to brothels with secret doors that allowed a thief in an adjacent room to reach in and filch from a client's coat or trousers when they were hung over a chair or in a closet. The rooms had trick locks that were easily opened from the outside. Thieves would slip in quietly while the patrons slept or were otherwise engaged and stole their valuables.

The Levee was often a violent place. The notorious Bucket of Blood saloon, for example, at 19th and Federal, was known for its brawls and, yes, blood. Across the street were a slew of brothels mostly occupied by African American girls and known as Bed Bug Row.

The Mickey Finn Special

Another famous Levee saloonkeeper was an Irishman by the name of Michael "Mickey" Finn. Between 1896 and 1903, he ran a saloon at 527 South State Street (now 1101 South State Street) in what was called Whiskey Row (another Whiskey Row was located near Ashland Avenue in the Back of the Yards). Like many newcomers, Finn came to Chicago during the World's Columbian Exposition. But Finn was no innocent greenhorn; he already had a trade. He was a skillful pickpocket and thief who recognized easy prey when he saw them, and he saw them plenty as they arrived at Dearborn Station in the heart of the Custom House Place Levee district. He worked at a rough-and-ready saloon in Little Cheyenne, which ran several blocks along South Clark Street, south of Van Buren. There he learned and improved his already remarkable "skills." Before long, he opened his own saloon, the Lone Star Saloon and Palm Garden. He was not only the owner; he also tended bar. It earned, and rightly so, its reputation as one of the roughest saloons in the city. It helped, too, that it served some of the strongest, most potent drinks.

One of those potent drinks was known as the "Mickey Finn Special," which consisted of a combination of raw alcohol, water and a mysterious powder. As the story goes, Finn at one point met a mysterious so-called voodoo priest by the name of Dr. Hall. Hall sold "love" potions to people in the vice district while also supplying them with heroin and cocaine. Finn purchased small brown bottles from the good "doctor," filled them with his own concoction and sold his unsuspecting customers the "Mickey Finn Special."

"The Mickey Finn Special" was the stiffest of drinks and had the desired effect: victims might appear at first talkative before falling into a deep sleep once the potion took effect. The ever-resourceful Finn employed so-called house girls who encouraged customers to drink as much as possible. Then the house girls and Finn himself (or perhaps another bartender), working in tandem, dragged the hapless victim into one of the saloon's back rooms, where he invariably would be stripped of his clothing and anything of value removed from his belongings. His body was then dumped in the alley behind the saloon.

Finn paid protection money to Hinky Dink and Bathhouse. They "took a portion of every dollar generated in the red-light district, through gambling or otherwise."[24] Rumors and stories of doping and various crimes eventually caught up with Finn. In December 1903, Mayor Carter Harrison Jr. shut down the Lone Star, even as Mickey's name and nefarious tactics persisted. His name is used generically to describe a drink laced with a drug in the phrase to "slip a mickey"—that is, to secretly drug someone. Years later, in July 1918, the *Chicago Tribune* was reporting about patrons being drugged with "Mickey Finn" powders in some of the city's finest restaurants, bars and hotels, including the Edelweiss, the Union League Club, the University Club, the Brevoort, the Bismarck Garden and the Green Mill. At the same

> ### THE LEVEE BY THE NUMBERS
>
> The First Ward statistics summed it up in a nutshell: by 1900, the Levee population was roughly five thousand, including 119 brothels staffed by nearly seven hundred women. According to the Vice Commission, the average age of the girls was twenty-three and a half, and the average professional life was five years. At its peak, the Levee population was fifty-five thousand, of whom roughly forty thousand were female.

time, Finn himself was up to his old antics when he was arrested in South Chicago for running a disorderly house.

The practice lives on still, or at least a variation of it. In October 2020, the *Tribune* reported that two Milwaukee women were accused of drugging ten men in River North and then robbing them of $85,000 worth of cash, phones and jewelry after they were unconscious.[25] The 2019 Jennifer Lopez film *Hustlers* was based on an article in *New York* magazine about New York City strippers who steal money from traders and CEOs by using their credit cards.

Today, there is a Mickey Finn's Brewery in Libertyville, which opened in 1994 and claims to be "the oldest brewpub in Illinois." The family-friendly brewery, though, has nothing in common with the original Mickey Finn except in name. It is housed in a one-hundred-year-old building in downtown Libertyville.

The Levee was also famous for its madams.

Madam Mary Hastings ran a brothel in Custom House Place that specialized in what the local press called white slavery. Today, we would say she engaged in sex trafficking.

It was a rough life for those who got caught in the middle of it. Hastings reportedly took in girls as young as thirteen, "broke" them in and sold them to other madams for $50 to $300 each.[26] She lured them to Chicago with promises of good jobs and good husbands and, once here, sold them to brothel keepers.

Vina Field's brothel was one of the few in the vice district run by an African American woman. She employed blond-haired Black prostitutes who serviced only white men and catered to a white male clientele and hired light-skinned Black girls and women and ran it, as one wag said, "as rigidly as a nunnery."

Another upscale madam was Carrie Watson. Her brownstone at 441 South Clark Street was considered "the show place" of the Levee. It boasted five parlors and a billiard room.

But the most famous madams of all were the Everleigh sisters, Ada and Minna. To say that their three-story, fifty-room mansion at 2131–33 South Dearborn Street was opulent is an understatement. It had its own string orchestras and no fewer than thirty boudoirs, "each with a mirrored ceiling and marble inlaid brass bed, a private bedroom with a tub laced in gold detailing, imported oil paintings, and hidden buttons that rang for champagne." It even had its own restaurant with a nationally known chef. The meals might feature fried oysters, Welsh rarebit, lobster and caviar. It boasted a floor-to-ceiling library, a huge ballroom with a water fountain and parquet floors, rare books, statuary, silk curtains and draperies, gilded bathtubs, gold-plated spittoons and a gold piano that cost $15,000. Altogether, twelve ornate soundproof parlors were contained under its roof, including Copper Room, Blue Room, Gold Room, Red Room, Green Room, Rose Room, Moorish Room, Egyptian Room and Chinese Room.

A Stranger Comes to Town

On October 28, 1893, the English investigative journalist and newspaper editor William T. Stead arrived in Chicago. It also happened to be the day a disappointed office seeker assassinated Carter Harrison Sr., the popular mayor, two days before the official end of the World's Columbian Exposition.

Hardly a good first impression.

Even though he lived thousands of miles away, like everyone else who read a newspaper, Stead had heard of Chicago and its wicked ways, its corruption and its notorious red-light district. Stirred by the paradoxical nature of the city—by its beauty, on the one hand, by its misery, on the other—he called Chicago "one of the wonders of the nineteenth century." During his visit, he made a concerted effort to see all aspects of the city—the good and the bad. But it is the bad that he is noted for. He dined with the wealthiest patrons who lived in their magnificent Prairie Avenue mansions, but he also conversed with the bartenders and madams and prostitutes in the Levee. He did his research.

A History of Brewing, Public Drinking and the Corner Bar

The garish cover of William F. Stead's sensational 1894 *If Christ Came to Chicago!* became the talk of the town. *Author collection.*

The result was a book that the city could not stop talking about.

In February 1894, Stead published his sensational four-hundred-page tome *If Christ Came to Chicago!* The garish cover said it all: a robed Christ figure, his left hand pointing a finger at a pack of locals rising from the debris of the ungodly city. The book reportedly sold seventy thousand copies on its first publication day alone.

He wrote about the cozy relationship between city hall and the city's gamblers and saloonkeepers, and he condemned the police department for its sheer lawlessness. What's more, he included a minutely detailed map—color coded, no less—of the city's vice district, the famous First Ward: its brothels, saloons, pawnshops and more. The appendix listed the addresses of the owners of the properties. Everything was there for the reader to see in plain sight.[27]

If anyone had any doubts about the infamy of the Levee, that notion was dispelled.

The First Ward Ball

Every year come December, Michael Kenna and John Coughlin organized a ball. But it wasn't just any ball.

It was the First Ward Ball.

The First Ward Ball was an annual political fundraiser. Held from 1896 to 1908, at its height as many as fifteen thousand people attended. It was a notorious example of Chicago at its most licentious. Initially, it was held at the Seventh Regiment Armory. Later, it moved to the larger Chicago Coliseum at 1513 South Wabash Avenue in what is now the South Loop. In addition to the First Ward Ball, the Coliseum also hosted Wild West shows, political conventions and later concerts and hockey matches (including the Chicago Blackhawks). In 1982, it was sold and partially demolished. The site is now occupied by the Buddhist organization Soka Gakkai USA Culture Center. Today, the Coliseum is commemorated with a modest park, Coliseum Park, at the corner of Wabash Avenue and 14th Place.

The origins of the First Ward Ball began one day during the Christmas season when Kenna and Coughlin were having a confab in Hinky Dink's saloon. Every year, they held an annual party for the "crippled" (to use the jargon of the time) Levee pianist and fiddler who went by the moniker of Lame Jimmy and worked at Carrie Watson's brothel. The annual gathering for the musician was usually held at Freiberg's Hall at 20 East 22nd Street (now Cermak Road—today the Hilliard Homes are located on the site), where police captains and regular beat cops mingled with the underworld. Although seemingly flush with cash, the aldermen were always looking for ways to add more to their coffers.

Then a thought occurred to Bathhouse. Why not hold a party at a larger venue not for one person but for the entire First Ward Democratic organization? They had plenty of friends who would be willing to contribute the libations. Everyone would be welcome. Everyone would come. It was a sure thing.

And they came.

Saloonkeepers, brewers, pimps, prostitutes, gamblers, pickpockets, thieves, politicians, police brass and various denizens of the First Ward all eagerly bought lots and lots of tickets. The Everleigh sisters, the grande dames of brothel owners, had their own private box. Typically, they drove up in their horse-drawn carriage. They were all there and all escorted by the police.

Because it was the first ball, Bathhouse John felt he had to wear something special to commemorate the event. Truth be told, Coughlin was a sight to be seen. He wore a green tailcoat, lavender trousers, a mauve vest, pink gloves and yellow shoes. Perched on his head was a silken top hat "that sparkled like the plate-glass windows of Marshall Field's department store." The highlight was the Grand March, which took place at the stroke of midnight, led by Kenna and followed by Coughlin, typically with an Everleigh sister on each arm.

It was a drunken revel and by all accounts a great success. Depending on the source, the First Ward Ball raised from $50,000 to $70,000 a year for the two aldermen through ticket sales and other concessions. Hinky Dink was so impressed with the first incarnation of the ball that he called it a "lallapalooza."[28]

Of course, not everyone was pleased. Church leaders condemned the ball as pushing beyond "all bounds of decency." Later balls were held in the even larger Coliseum, where, at one point, some twenty thousand guests reportedly drank ten thousand quarts of champagne and thirty thousand quarts of beer. Over the years, it became coarser and the behavior more outrageous. "Riotous drunks had stripped off the costumes of unattended young women, maudlin inebriates collapsed in the aisles, a madam…stabbed her boy friend with a hat pin, several toughs suffered broken jaws…and a thirty-five-foot bar was smashed to bits in one of a hundred free-for-all fights."[29]

Over the years, there were various attempts to bring the First Ward Ball to an end and shut down the Levee altogether, especially after Nathaniel Ford Moore, a golfer and son of the president of the Rock Island Railway Company, died in Victoria "Vic" Shaw's brothel of a narcotics overdose. Most sensational of all, though, was the death in late 1905 of thirty-seven-year-old Marshall Field Jr., son of the department store merchant. Field, a married man and the father of three at the time, died of a gunshot wound after a prostitute reportedly shot him at the Everleigh Club.

In October 1909, Rodney "Gipsy" Smith, an English evangelist, led an anti–white slavery parade in the Levee district. Thousands—reports of tens of thousands, according to some accounts—joined Smith in song, performing hymns and listening to his fire-and-brimstone preaching. Then a Salvation Army band led the throng into the heart of the Levee singing such songs as "Where Is My Wandering Boy Tonight?" and "Where He Leads Me I Will Follow." The residents of the Levee played along to appease the crowd, dimming their lights and quieting the music, but once Smith and his coterie left, the lights went back on as usual and everyone resumed their raucous ways.

But each year, the protests continued and became increasingly more intense. At one point, the Woman's Christian Temperance Union marched through the downtown streets and demanded that Mayor Fred Busse stop the next year's ball. It would have been a simple procedure. All he had to do was refuse the aldermen a liquor license. This was at a time when the suffrage movement was garnering attention in Chicago and throughout the United States.

Bowing to the pressure, finally, in March 1910, Busse announced the establishment of a Vice Commission to investigate Chicago's "social evil" problem. The members included some of the city's most prominent citizens, including Julius Rosenwald, president of Sears, Roebuck & Co. Chairman Dean Sumner and his fellow colleagues interviewed not only saloonkeepers and madams but also victims of white slavery and prostitutes.

On April 5, 1911, the thirty-member commission issued their report to the city council, a damning and shocking indictment consisting of some 400 pages. Everything was there for the world to see: prostitution, drugs, murder. It wasn't the content that was surprising. It was the sheer volume of it—and all presented at once under one cover. It listed 1,020 resorts, operated by 1,800 madams and housing at least 4,000 prostitutes. The annual profits from crime and vice in the Levee differed depending on the source. According to Wendt and Kogan, the revenue amounted to $60 million per year. Abbott says it was more like an annual $16 million (or $328 million in today's dollars).[30] Either way, it was a huge and embarrassing sum, which prompted the commission to call for the "extermination" of the vice district.

Thus, by the time the anti-vice crusades closed the red-light district in the Levee in 1912, public drinking in a saloon was no longer deemed respectable. Moreover, the hothouse flower atmosphere of the Levee was considered nothing less than a public health issue. "Public health officials claimed that the liquor served in saloons was adulterated with artificial coloring."[31]

Around the same time, Minna Everleigh was trying to pump up business by hiring a professional photographer to take photos of the club to be used for a discreet and tasteful brochure, *The Everleigh Club, Illustrated*, bound in an elegant leather cover. Minna herself wrote an introduction. She referred to the brochure as a "little booklet" that will "convey but a faint idea of the magnificence of the club." She sent the "booklet" to nearly two hundred regular and prospective clients.[32]

The timing could not have been worse.

Cold Beer and Hot Graft:
The Day a Newspaper Bought a Bar

The building that stands at 731 North Wells Street has been around for a long time and has housed numerous businesses, from a linen supply company to a restaurant. In 1980, two brothers with the surname of Burke opened what is now the Brehon Pub (named after Brehon law, an early form of Irish jurisdiction that dated back to the Iron Age). It's a handsome place and remains a popular watering hole to this day. Most people who walk by it have no idea of the role the structure played in the history of Chicago bar culture.

A few years earlier, in 1977, a major Chicago newspaper, the *Sun-Times*, did the unthinkable. It bought a bar—the bar that is now the Brehon Pub—and called it the aptly named Mirage, for that's exactly what it was. Reporters from the *Sun-Times* investigated allegations of official corruption and shakedowns against small businesses by city officials in order to document city inspectors taking kickbacks and payoffs for ignoring health and safety code violations. At other times, state liquor inspectors were caught skimming taxes. It involved small amounts ranging from ten to twenty-five dollars, from plumbing inspectors, building inspectors, electric inspectors and fire inspectors. Ultimately, the sting led to some thirty-four convictions.

In May 1977, journalist Pam Zekman and BGA investigator Bill Recktenwald posed as a married couple, Pam and Ray Patterson. They "purchased" the tavern with a $5,000 down payment on an $18,000 asking price. It was all very hush-hush. A fellow reporter, Zay N. Smith, wrote the series and pretended to be the bartender, while another BGA investigator, Jeff Allen, posed as the manager.

Throughout it all, the reporters took copious notes and maintained a meticulous diary. Photographer Jim Frost surreptitiously took photographs using a rigged-up ventilation opening where he could shoot the nefarious activities without being noticed. Since none of them had any experience behind a bar, Smith attended bartending school to learn the trade well enough to appear convincing.

> Altogether, the Mirage existed for just four months. But during that time, the reporters collected enough evidence to reveal a widespread culture of corruption, including tax fraud that cost the city $16 million annually.
>
> In 1978, the *Sun-Times* published a twenty-five-part series on the Mirage that was nominated for the Pulitzer Prize for general reporting. (In a bit of post-Watergate irony, *Washington Post* editor Benjamin Bradlee, a member of the Pulitzer board, condemned the reporters for using deception to get their story. He claimed it smacked of entrapment and was thus not worthy of a Pulitzer. In particular, Bradlee asserted that the journalists were misrepresenting themselves.)
>
> The impact was severe: more than a dozen officials were suspended or fired; inspectors were convicted of bribery. Ultimately, Mayor Michael Bilandic created an Office of Professional Review, and the Illinois Department of Revenue created a task force to uncover tax fraud.

The Everleigh Club was an embarrassment and an ongoing reminder of the prominent role vice played in Chicago for the Carter Harrison administration (who was the son of the murdered mayor). Everybody knew about the Everleigh Club, but the conversation around it, at least in public, was supposed to be discreet. Now here was this brochure for all to see. Harrison even had his own copy of it on his desk. He couldn't ignore it any longer.

On October 24, 1911, Harrison announced that the Everleigh Club would be shut down.[33] Still, not everything closed. Many establishments lingered for several years. Freiberg's, for example, didn't close its doors until August 2014.

The Levee lived on in other ways, too. Some of the old places were transformed into cabarets or given new names. Ike Bloom's infamous dance hall, for example, was renamed Old Vienna before it became the equally famous Midnight Frolics.

A History of Brewing, Public Drinking and the Corner Bar

End of an Era

"Bathhouse John" Coughlin died in November 1938, "and over the seat Alderman Coughlin had occupied for forty-six years" his former colleagues "spread black and purple crepe, and on his desk they set a vase of roses."[34] To keep continuity, the party bosses asked the retired eighty-year-old Michael Kenna to return to the city council and take over Coughlin's seat. He wouldn't have to do much, they insisted; just attend ward meetings. So he did, although he never said a word. His presence was enough. Then, after a while, he stopped coming altogether, preferring to stay in the soothing confines of his Auditorium Hotel suite, one of the several hotels he lived in during his later years. He died in 1946 at the Blackstone Hotel of diabetes and myocarditis.

By then, of course, Kenna and Coughlin's heyday was long over. As early as the 1920s, Kenna and Coughlin's influence was ebbing as a new and more violent generation such as James "Big Jim" Colosimo and Johnny Torrio vied for control of vice in the city and began to administer the First Ward coffers.

A new day was coming. Kenna and Coughlin were relics of another era.

The Hinky Drink

Courtesy of WTTW's *Chicago Tonight*

¾ ounce fresh lime juice
¼ ounce ginger syrup
¼ ounce orgeat
½ ounce Curacao
1½ ounces amber rum
¼ ounce Jamaican rum

In a cocktail mixer filled with ice, shake all ingredients but the Jamaican rum and strain into a rocks glass. Float the Jamaican over the top using an upside-down spoon. Garnish with a lime round.*

* Erica Gunderson, "Original Chicago Cocktail: The Hinky Drink," WTTW website, May 13, 2016.

First Ward Ball Revival

The program from a reenactment of the First Ward Ball, presented by the Chicago branch of Atlas Obscura and held in Chicago's South Loop. *Photo by author.*

In January 2019, the Chicago chapter of Atlas Obscura, the online magazine and travel company, presented a reinvention of the First Ward Ball at a South Loop bar, the Bassline. It featured entertainment, drag performers, burlesque dancers and lectures by Adam Selzer, Liz Garibay and Paul Dailing, as well as poker and blackjack games.[35] But this wasn't the first time the event was brought back to life. A few years earlier, on March 17, 2013, Pocket Guide to Hell sponsored an reenactment at the Hideout on Wabansia. The evening featured live music, dancing, food and drink, as well as a charming poster by Sara Jean Cough.

Chapter 3
TEMPERANCE, PROHIBITION AND ORGANIZED CRIME

Sometimes it seems that the only thing Prohibition managed to do was spur people do drink even harder. When you're breaking the law, it sure makes your mouth dry.
—Dana Jennings, Sing Me Back Home: Love, Death, and Country Music

I make my money by supplying a public demand.
—Al Capone

Prohibition was the noble experiment that failed in spectacular fashion. During its fourteen years of existence, there was *more* crime, not less. Rather than reducing crime and bringing the family together, Prohibition led to social upheaval and, what's more, created organized crime syndicates, all the while, notes Daniel Okrent, depriving the government of much-needed revenue. It encouraged bribery, blackmail and all varieties of corruption.[36]

There were other paradoxes. People still drank during Prohibition. Prohibition may have banned the sale of beer, but that didn't mean that people had to stop making it or drinking it. Prohibition didn't close all the breweries, but it did reduce the number significantly. Thus, Prohibition may have reduced brewery output, but it certainly didn't reduce the *demand* for beer. According to Bob Skilnik, five breweries in Chicago stayed open by producing "near beer."[37] When Al Capone got involved, he added more alcohol to the mix, creating something called "needle beer." Near beer is just what it sounds like: beer with alcoholic content that is not quite strong enough to qualify as beer. Needle beer was made with illicit alcohol under precarious conditions.

Prohibition occurred for several reasons, but much of it revolved around anti-immigration—anti-Catholic sentiment in particular played its part—and especially a pronounced hostility toward German and Irish saloonkeepers. Reformers such as Frances Willard of the WCTU looked askance at the "infidel" origins of so many of the country's saloonkeepers.[38]

Ostensibly, Prohibition was intended to reduce crime and corruption, to solve social problems and to improve both the physical and mental health of Americans. The Prohibition and anti-alcohol movements were linked to various other movements, including women's suffrage. Women reformers associated drunkenness and social disorder in general with destructive male behavior and forged an alliance with the movers and shakers in the prohibition and temperance movements, which had a profound effect on American life. As Susan Cheever notes, "If men were irresponsible, Prohibition came to be seen as the answer."[39] Many of the national suffrage leaders also supported temperance, including Susan B. Anthony and Elizabeth Cady Stanton. Consequently, temperance and women's suffrage became intertwined in the public consciousness.

Thus, Prohibition may have had good intentions—to improve the overall well-being of Americans—but its execution was disastrous, and the end result had a deleterious effect on both the brewing and tavern industries.

Saloon Culture Pre-Prohibition

The pre-Prohibition saloon—or the old-time saloon, as George Ade called it—played a key cultural and historical role in the life of the city. Its heyday was from the early 1870s to 1920. At its best, the saloon embodied the "rooster crow of the spirit of democracy," as Ade so colorfully put it.[40] For the ordinary man (if not woman), the saloon was his public space, his home away from home. Paradoxically, it brought people together even when its many critics asserted it attributed to the overall decline of the social fabric.

The saloon offered more than companionship and a place to get away from the encroaching urbanization that enveloped America's biggest cities. It had its practical aspects too. Saloonkeepers cashed checks, offered a helping hand to those in need or received mail. Sometimes the saloon functioned as a ramshackle inn, providing a place to rest one's head for a small price.

> ### THE WHITECHAPEL CLUB
>
> Chicago has had its share of unconventional journalists, but none were quite as notorious as the members of the Whitechapel Club, a social organization that thumbed its collective nose at the hypocrisy of respectable society and took its name from the rough London neighborhood where Jack the Ripper found his unwilling victims. Appropriately enough, the members gathered in the back room of Henry Koster's saloon on Calhoun Place, also known as Newsboys' Alley. The qualifications for membership were "wit and good fellowship," but the real purpose of their get-togethers was "serious drinking and newspaper gossip." They told stories, recited favorite poems or perhaps read from a work in progress, culminating in a round of jovial drinking songs.
>
> The Whitechapel Club was renowned for its gleefully macabre ambiance, which included various skulls and hangman's nooses that adorned its walls and ceilings. But the chief focus was the huge coffin-shaped dining table. Its members included the reporter Finley Peter Dunne, humorists George Ade and Opie Read and cartoonist John T. McCutcheon. Guests included Theodore Roosevelt, poet James Whitcomb Riley and boxers James J. Corbett and John L. Sullivan. Even William T. Stead, author of the sensational *If Christ Came to Chicago!*, stopped by.

Often, saloons provided the only public toilets, or "comfort stations," as they were sometimes called. And for the price of a nickel, patrons not only got a beer but also were offered a free lunch, which could range from the humble (pickles, pretzels, crackers) to the generous (egg sandwiches, potatoes, vegetables, hot and cold meats, a cheese spread). "The poor saw free lunches as a blessing, even a necessity," offers Bill Savage.[41] Supporters of the practice viewed it as a form of social welfare. On the other hand, its detractors dismissed it as nothing more than an attempt to get working-class men to part with their hard-earned money while their wives and children waited at home—the lunch may have ostensibly been "free," but the men still spent precious time away.

Temperance and a Woman Named Frances Willard

One of the leading figures of the anti-alcohol movement was Frances Willard, co-founder of the Woman's Christian Temperance Union. The WCTU had midwestern roots, established in Cleveland, Ohio, in 1874, with the purpose of creating a "sober and pure world" that advocated for abstinence and purity under the watchful eye of evangelical Christianity. Its constitution called for the prohibition of "the manufacture and sale of intoxicating liquors as a beverage." Annie Wittenmyer was the organization's first president, but Willard took over in 1879 and turned the WCTU into the largest organization of women in the world at the time, as well as one of the most effective political action groups of the nineteenth century or, indeed, of any era. Daniel Okrent refers to Willard as "propagandist" and "chief technician," as well as "nearly a deity to a 250,000-member army."[42] Among the forms of protest of the WCTU members was going to saloons and kneeling on the floors while singing Christian hymns.[43] But there was more to the WCTU than just denouncing alcohol; there were also social service and educational programs. It advocated for prison reform, free kindergarten, vocational schools, the eight-hour day and workers' rights. Willard thought of herself as no less than a Christian socialist.[44]

Willard was born in a village outside Rochester, New York, of sturdy New England stock and raised on a farm outside Janesville, Wisconsin, before moving with her parents to the "Methodist heaven" of Evanston, Illinois, just north of Chicago. Even as a teen, she condemned the consumption of alcohol. As the leader of the WCTU, she viewed temperance as not only a woman's issue but also a moral issue: it was up to the women of America to rescue the country from the evils of demon alcohol. The elimination of alcohol from American homes was necessary to maintain the health and welfare—moral and physical—of the American family. But temperance was not enough. What Willard really wanted was for liquor to be outlawed outright or, if that was unlikely, at least some form of prohibition.

Prominent figures of the progressive movement believed they could make immigrant lives better by weaning them off what they considered the evil effects of alcohol. Jane Addams, one of the founders of Chicago's Hull House, supported Prohibition even as she understood the reasons behind the popularity of the saloon. She inherently recognized and acknowledged its appeal, the warmth and affability it fostered among people, but she also felt that its evils outweighed its benefits.

On the other hand, the fiery preacher and former Chicago White Stockings baseball player Billy Sunday had no sympathy whatsoever toward the saloon or the saloonkeeper. Sunday was as popular in his own day as Billy Graham was in ours: a 1914 magazine poll placed Sunday as the eighth-greatest man in the United States, tying with industrialist Andrew Carnegie. He traveled across the country preaching to millions of people and using "plain Anglo-Saxon words" to get his message across to the ordinary workingman and woman—the kind of people (without the women, of course) who would typically frequent saloons. Liquor, he proclaimed, was the enemy, and those who profited from the sale of alcohol were no better than Satan himself.[45] (Ironically, Billy Sunday, the Logan Square cocktail bar, is named after him.)

In his book *Gossip Men*, Christopher Elias observes that the overwhelming focus of the reformist and temperance organizations and groups was the "regulation of male morality": in order to improve the status and well-being of women and children—that is, the family—one had to "curb the drinking of men." Reducing male drinking and drunkenness would also reduce, advocates believed, the number of rapes and incidents of domestic violence, as well as lead fewer women to prostitution. No less than FBI director J. Edgar Hoover promulgated such beliefs. If successful, temperance would "reaffirm" the patriarchal hierarchy within the family and in the broader American society.[46]

THE ANTI-SALOON LEAGUE

The Anti-Saloon League (ASL) was another prominent temperance group established in the Midwest, in Oberlin, Ohio, in 1893. As its name implies, it focused exclusively on the demise of the saloon. During its heyday, its members numbered in the millions. An early example of a successful pressure group, its leadership knew how to wield power and what tactics to use to get what it wanted. Unlike Willard's scattered "Do Everything" approach, Howard Hyde Russell, who first organized the Ohio branch before helming the national chapter, used intimidation and a clear-eyed focus to concentrate on the Prohibition effort, supported largely but not exclusively by Protestant churches and congregations; the leadership and staff of the ASL were overwhelmingly Methodist and Baptist.[47]

The leaders of the organization were interested in expanding their scope outside Ohio and thus set their sights on other cities, including Chicago, which many members considered the epitome of depravity, wickedness and sin, being well aware of the city's notorious Levee district. It was a city, they maintained, built on corruption, gambling, prostitution and other vices—and those vices were fueled by alcohol. Initially, the ASL concentrated its efforts on Sunday saloon closings, an ongoing issue among city leaders. The influence and pressure of the Evanston-based WCTU added to the momentum.

Political cartoons and advertising campaigns railed against the social disorder and damage that drinking in saloons had on American families. Rather than attending to wives and children, said critics, fathers preferred to spend their leisurely hours drinking in saloons. Saloons were condemned as being havens for gambling, prostitution and corruption and were the frequent object of the sensational press. The league was a major force in politics and contributed to the passage of Prohibition in 1919. The league also encouraged the passage of local option laws that allowed individual wards or cities to vote themselves dry.

Local Options

In 1894, Chicago City Council allowed aldermen to designate small residential areas of their wards as so-called anti-saloon territory, also referred to as the local option. More than a decade later, in 1907, the Illinois legislature allowed voters to turn entire precincts dry. By 1909, nearly two-thirds of the city was dry. This meant that since so many neighborhoods voted themselves dry, many saloons were concentrated in the Loop, in working-class neighborhoods or in the slums. As recently as 1995, the local option allowed voters to prohibit liquor sales at specific addresses. Chicago has become drier over the decades and remains so: "By 2003 nearly one-fifth of Chicago's more than 2,700 precincts restricted the sale of alcohol."[48]

Reformers Have Their Say

The Prohibition movement started after the Civil War. In September 1869, the Chicago chapter of the Prohibition Party was founded. Members opposed the sale or consumption of alcohol. One of the major objectives of prohibitionists and temperance movement leaders was to close taverns on Sunday.

Pursuing Sunday closing laws was not a new phenomenon. But the attempts often led to more trouble than they were worth, as indicated by the chaos that erupted during the Lager Beer Riot of 1855 (previously discussed in chapter 2). More often than not, the laws, though they were on the books, were simply ignored until circumstances—there were too many saloons and leading to too much social disorder—dictated otherwise.

Thus, under growing pressure, the local media also joined the reform bandwagon, suggesting one way of decreasing the number of saloons was to raise the license fee. Such an increase, critics maintained, would not only reduce the number but also appease the reformers and the growing prohibition movement.

The politicians were listening too as the anti-alcohol and anti-vice reform movement continued to gain steam. In 1906, the city council issued a liquor fee increase that went into effect in May. As a result, of the 7,600 saloons at the time, more than 1,300 shut down.[49] These and other measures, though, did not completely satisfy the reformers. Instead, they expressed their dismay with a prohibition march on September 26, 1908, in downtown Chicago.

Responding to the pressure, political leaders reconsidered the Sunday closing laws. Mayor Bill Thompson, who had pledged as a mayoral candidate not to close saloons on Sundays, did an about-face and proclaimed that starting on October 9, 1915, Chicago saloons would indeed be closed on the Sabbath. Prior to this, Chicago mayors tended to turn a blind eye toward Sunday closings through non-enforcement or outright ignoring of it.

Saloon patrons did not accept the closings without putting up a fight. In response, Anton Cermak and his United Societies Party sponsored a "wet" parade that consisted of fifty thousand to seventy thousand supporters who marched downtown in protest. Reporters couldn't help but notice that the wet parade had a much larger turnout than previous dry parades.[50] Participants included not only German immigrants and members of the German American community and German organizations but also people who felt their personal liberty was under attack.

In April 1917, the United States declared war on Germany during World War I. It led to a growing resentment and anger toward the German American community, which led, in turn, to a resurgence of nativist sentiments that resembled the Know Nothing Party of the nineteenth century. Drinking beer during World War I, especially beer made by German brewers, became an unpatriotic act. The Anti-Saloon League, in particular, viewed predominantly German breweries as un-American.

Chicago Beer

Beer Gardens and a Bar Named Berghoff

Before the advent of World War I, Chicago had a rich German drinking culture. German immigrants brought their beloved beer gardens with them to the United States. Beer gardens and beer halls offered a taste of home. These beer gardens also served as community centers and settings for civic, social and political activities and organizations.

The first lager beer garden was opened in Chicago in 1847 by German immigrant John Huck and his business partner, John Schneider, and was adjacent to his brewery. Huck and Schneider served lager beer, not the heavier ales or stouts that were more common in Irish American taverns or taverns operated by native-born Americans. Also unlike Irish taverns, German beer gardens were family-friendly outdoor spaces. They offered music, games and other forms of entertainment, serving typical German fare such as pretzels with mustard, liverwurst and bratwurst. Some even resembled amusement parks. More importantly, they provided a sense of community and reminded German immigrants of the customs and traditions they left behind.

Among the most famous was the Rainbo Gardens at 4812–36 North Clark Street. Rainbo presented a mixture of vaudeville acts, jazz bands, sporting events and dancing. It featured a two-story beer hall, a bowling alley, an outdoor dance floor and refreshment stands. It could accommodate up to two thousand diners. Some of the biggest names in entertainment performed there, including Isham Jones and his orchestra. Like many venues, Prohibition adversely affected the Rainbo Gardens. But even though alcohol was banned, patrons smuggled flasks of liquor under the not-so-watchful eyes of Rainbo's managers, who chose to ignore the flagrant violations. Even so, the Rainbo was raided off and on during the Prohibition era. It came to a head in 1928, when federal authorities ordered the venue shut down. It eventually reopened under various owners and under various guises; it has held wrestling matches and been turned into a bowling alley. An ice skating rink was installed in 1957. More recently, rock concerts were held there.

Equally famous was the Bismarck Gardens located at the southwest corner of Grace and Halsted in Lakeview. Opened in 1895 by the brothers Emil and Karl Eitel, the Bismarck Gardens became one of the most popular beer gardens in the city with its shady trees, electric lamps, outdoor stage and dance floor. It also featured a year-round beer hall that highlighted German bands. It was renamed Marigold Gardens in 1915 due to the rising anti-German sentiment during World War I.

A History of Brewing, Public Drinking and the Corner Bar

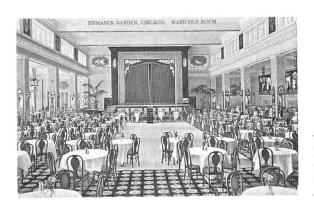

The Marigold Room of the Bismarck Gardens, one of the finest beer gardens in the city at the time. *Author collection.*

One of Chicago's early amusement parks had beer garden roots: Sans Souci Amusement Park, at 6000 South Cottage Grove Avenue. Although it opened in the summer of 1899, its origins date to the World's Columbian Exposition of 1893 and the popularity of the Midway Plaisance, a mile-long stretch of amusements, eateries, theaters and the original Ferris wheel between Jackson and Washington Parks in the Hyde Park neighborhood. But Sans Souci's immediate predecessor was Old Vienna, a roadside refreshment stand and German beer garden that opened a year after the fair, in 1894. Encouraged by its success, a group of investors acquired Old Vienna with the idea of expanding it and turning it into an amusement park. Dubbed Sans Souci after Frederick the Great's palace, it resembled the exterior of a German beer hall and, like other German beer gardens, included shady trees, but it also boasted a Japanese tea garden, ornamental shrubbery, electric fountains and evening lighting. Its biggest attraction, though, was the Casino, where patrons could eat and drink al fresco while listening to bands and orchestras.

In 1914, the owners replaced Sans Souci with an upscale indoor/outdoor entertainment complex called the Midway Gardens designed by Frank Lloyd Wright. It was intended to be part European-style concert garden and part German beer hall that included year-round dining, drinking and entertainment, including the Midway Gardens Orchestra. Due to financial problems, in 1916 it was purchased by Schoenhofen Brewery and renamed Edelweiss Gardens. It remained open as a dry establishment during Prohibition. But a combination of anti-German sentiment and the ongoing effects of Prohibition led to its being demolished in 1929.

Beer gardens are still a part of Chicago drinking culture, if not quite so grand. Pubs with noteworthy beer gardens include Chief O'Neill's in Avondale, Sheffield's Beer and Wine Garden in Lakeview, Resi's Bierstube

Sans Souci Amusement Park at the corner of 60th Street and Cottage Grove Avenue. The park had its roots in the German beer garden tradition. *Author collection.*

in North Center, Half Acre Brewery in Bowmanville and Moody's Pub in Edgewater. District Brew Yards in River West features the beer of three breweries—Burnt City, Around the Bend and Bold Dog—as well as an adjacent beer garden.

AMONG THE MOST FAMOUS and historic German breweries—and still very much a part of the beer scene—is the Berghoff.

German immigrant Herman Berghoff opened the Berghoff in 1898, serving his own Dortmunder-style beer for five cents a glass and ten cents a stein, along with a free corned beef sandwich. Herman's sons expanded the menu and added stained-glass windows and murals. During Prohibition, the Berghoff survived by selling near beer and its own line of soda drinks, and when Prohibition ended in 1933, Herman Berghoff was famously the first to obtain a retail liquor license.

In 2018, the Berghoff Restaurant opened a craft beer brewery, Adams Street Brewery, on site.

Chicago has had other German taverns of import. Despite being one of the most popular German bierstubes, Zum Deutschen Eck at 2914 North Southport Avenue closed abruptly in early 2000. Housed in a handsome

The interior of the Berghoff as it looked in the 1920s. *Author collection.*

half-timbered Tudor-style building, it featured German sing-alongs on weekends and was known for its hospitality and warm atmosphere. A plaque commemorates the former site.

Schulien's at 2100 West Irving Park Road in North Center originally opened in 1886 in Lincoln Park. During Prohibition, it was a speakeasy, but it was popular for another reason. In the 1920s, the Schulien family hired magicians to perform magic tricks at diners' tables. It closed in early 1999 and is now O'Donovan's, a neighborhood bar. Matt Igler's was a German restaurant at 1627–29 West Melrose Street near the busy intersection of Belmont, Ashland and Lincoln that not only served hearty German fare but also featured singing German waiters.

Chicago Brauhaus has a happier ending. For more than fifty years, Chicago Brauhaus in Lincoln Square served huge steins of beer and brats at 4732 North Lincoln Avenue before shutting down in 2017. In September 2020, DANK Haus German American Cultural Center created a replica of the long-running bar on the second floor of the 1927 building.

The Prohibition Era Begins

In 1918, Congress passed the Eighteenth Amendment, which declared the transportation, manufacture and sale of "intoxicating liquor" illegal in the United States. But it took the Volstead Act, passed in October 1919 and which went into effect on January 7, 1920, to actually enforce it. Drinking itself was not prohibited—only the sale, manufacture and transportation of alcohol. Some alcoholic beverages, such as so-called near beer, as well as sacramental wine, remained legal. It was also legal to store and drink alcohol at home.

During the early years of Prohibition, numerous breweries switched from brewing beer to manufacturing non-beer products in order to survive. Schoenhofen, for example, made Green River Soda. Others made so-called cereal beverages (Atlas, Birk Brothers, Independent, McAvoy, Best, Conrad Seipp, Stenson and United). Cereal beverage referred to a drink that was produced either wholly or in part from malt (or a substitute for malt) and either fermented or unfermented, which contains, when ready for consumption, less than one-half of 1 percent of alcohol by volume. Still others made root beer or turned to cold storage.[51]

The problem for supporters of Prohibition was that by and large, Chicagoans opposed it. The brewers themselves were especially concerned that they would lose their livelihoods. But they were willing to take the risk of returning to the manufacture of beer if someone was willing to protect them from arrest and prosecution. In sum, Prohibition reduced Chicago breweries from more than forty to fewer than twenty. Organized crime helped those that remained get over the hump.

From Colosimo to Torrio to O'Banion to Capone

Prohibition changed everything for Michael "Hinky Dink" Kenna. By the summer of 1919, he saw the writing on the wall. That July 1, his South Loop tavern, the Workingmen's Exchange, anticipating the changes in the law, sold the legal near beer, but it wasn't the same. Six months later, he decided to shut it down and transformed it into a candy, sandwich and cigar store—but not before he gave away a few of his famous schooners, including one to Mayor Bill Thompson and another to the Chicago Historical Society (now the Chicago History Museum).[52] As an aside, the schooners were eight inches

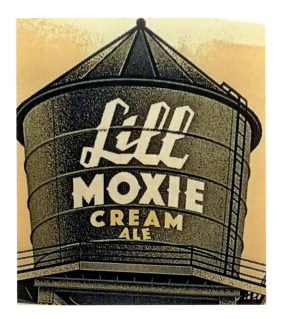

Top, left: Lill Moxie Cream Ale. Flagship brand of Lill & Diversey (also spelled Diversy).

Top, right: As part of the "History of American Breweries" series, Wisconsin-based Huber Brewing released a collectable beer can honoring Lill & Diversey. According to the label, "Lill & Diversey became one of the largest breweries in the Midwest and 'Lill's Cream Ale' was one of the most famous brands in the country."

Bottom: A historic advertisement from circa 1862 of Lill & Diversy (notice spelling) promoting its premium ale, pale ale, stock ale, porter and other brews. *Author collection.*

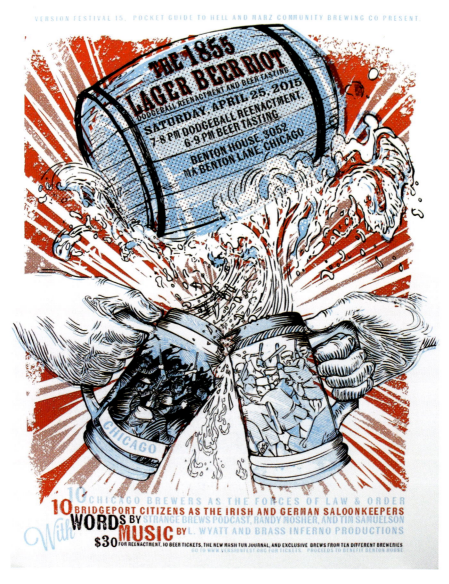

"The 1855 Lager Beer Riot" poster. On April 25, 2015, Paul Durica's Pocket Guide to Hell and Marz Community Brewing presented a dodgeball reenactment (and beer tasting) of the Lager Beer Riot at Benton House in the Bridgeport neighborhood of Chicago. Participants included brewmaster and craft brewing genius Randy Mosher, Chicago cultural historian Tim Samuelson and Northwestern University professor Bill Savage. *Artwork by Kathleen Judge.*

The Coliseum as it would have appeared around the time of Kenna and Coughlin's First Ward Ball. *Theresa K. Albini collection.*

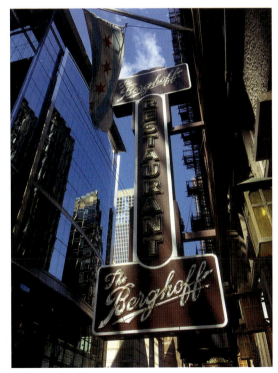

The Berghoff restaurant has been serving traditional German cuisine and steins of beer since 1898. *Photo by author.*

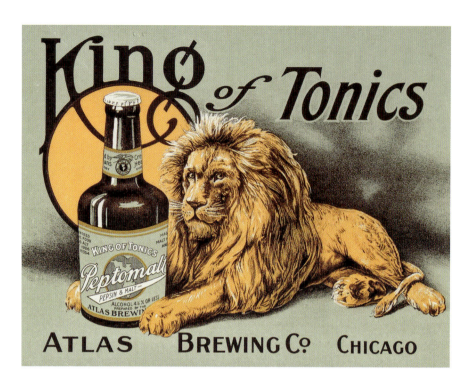

Above: King of Tonics. The king of the jungle cradles Atlas Brewing's Peptomalt tonic. *Author collection.*

Left: Goose Island's taproom on Clybourn Avenue. *Photo by author.*

Moody Tongue's deconstructed cheesecake consists of mango sorbet, passion fruit curd, pine nut crumble and pineapple conserva. *Photo by Theresa K. Albini.*

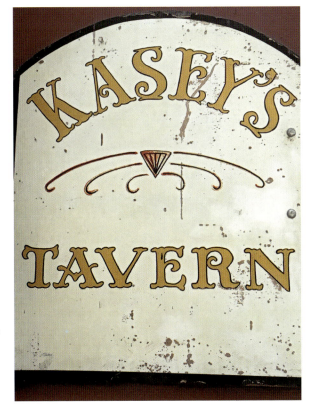

The back door of Kasey's Tavern, the epitome of the corner bar even though it is not actually on a corner. At Kasey's, everyone knows your name or at least recognizes your face. As Bill Savage once told me, "Bars are where people tell each other secrets." *Photo by author.*

Whiskey Row referred to a stretch of taverns that quenched the thirst of slaughterhouse workers who labored at Chicago's Union Stock Yards. *Author collection.*

The BEER sign once graced the window of Half Acre Brewery at its Lincoln Avenue location. In 2021, it was announced that Hop Butcher for the World planned to move into the space. Meanwhile, Half Acre's brewery, taproom and beer garden remains open on Balmoral Avenue. *Photo by author.*

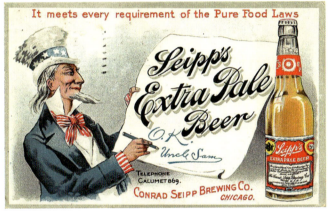

Top: A typically extravagant and colorful Conrad Seipp ad in honor of the 1893 World's Columbian Exposition.

Middle: Seipp's Extra Pale Beer and Uncle Sam agree: Seipp's Extra Pale Ale "meets every requirement of the Pure Food Laws." Seipp's current motto is, "Just a little better than the kind you thought was best."

Bottom: "You can't get around it. It's the pure food beer." *Author collection.*

Greenstar Brewing, housed in the Uncommon Ground coffeehouse/restaurant space on Clark Street, was the first all–certified organic brewery in Illinois. Its mission is not only to "do good beer" but also to have a "do good beer" program. *Photo by author.*

Jolly Pumpkin in Hyde Park is the first Chicago location for the Dexter, Michigan–based brewery and the first all–sour, all–oak aged brewery in the United States. Michigan-based artist Adam Forman has been creating the haunting, often fantastical labels for Jolly Pumpkin since 2004. His work has been described as a mash-up of disparate styles ranging from the French posters of Toulouse-Lautrec to the whimsy of Lewis Carroll. *Photo by author.*

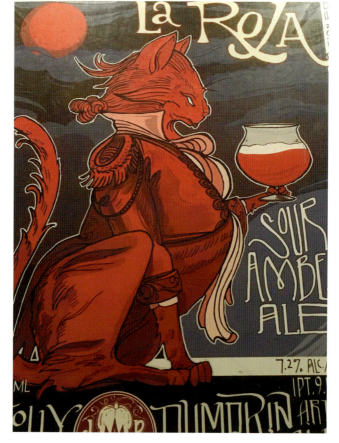

Coffeehouse and bakery by day, brewpub and pizzeria by night (although beer is always available no matter what the time), Middle Brow's motto is "Drink good. Do better." As the name indicates, Middle Brow is a socially conscious brewer: a substantial amount of its profits goes to such charities as the Greater Chicago Food Depository and Ceasefire. The taproom, Bungalow, is named in honor of the iconic but humble Chicago bungalow, of which there are roughly eighty thousand scattered throughout the city. *Photo by author.*

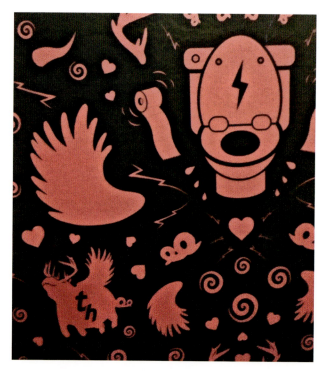

"Embrace your strange" is Twisted Hippo's motto. Indeed, strangeness and wacky humor are apparent in the brewery's beers (Velvet Elvis is an ale that features peanut butter, banana and bacon) and even its whimsical restrooms, as pictured here. *Photo by author.*

Marz Community Brewing Company emphasizes the "community" in its name. Marz is dedicated to making small, artisanal batches of beer in a sustainable and socially responsible manner. Then they share what they've made with "our families, community, and friends we have yet to meet." *Courtesy of Marz.*

The handsome structure that houses Schubas Tavern at the corner of Belmont and Southport Avenues is one of the original Schlitz buildings in the city. Designed in a German Renaissance Revival style, it features multicolored brickwork, a bonnet roof and the distinctive Schlitz logo with its belted globe. *Photo by Theresa K. Albini.*

Schoenhofen's "Jumping on to something good" ad, circa 1910. Frogs, trees and a basket of beer. What more could you ask for? *Author collection.*

Top: Established in 1934, Simon's Tavern must have the best bar signage in the city, or certainly the most distinctive: bright blue and yellow—the colors of Sweden—depicting a happy-looking "pickled herring" holding a martini. The traditional Nordic glögg is served year-round: in the winter typically with raisins, almonds and pepparkakor, and in the summer as a slushie. This bar has great murals and a jukebox too. *Photo by author.*

Bottom: The Chicago Brewseum's first exhibition, *Brewing Up Chicago: How Beer Transformed a City*, ended its run at the Field Museum on January 5, 2020. *Photo by author.*

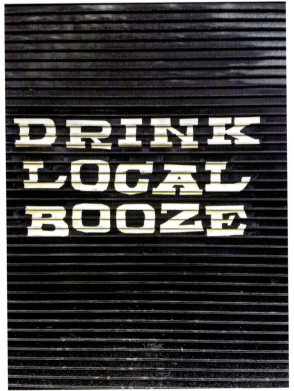

Above: Daisy Cutter Pale Ale, Half Acre's flagship brew. *Photo by author.*

Left: Drink Local Booze. *Photo by author.*

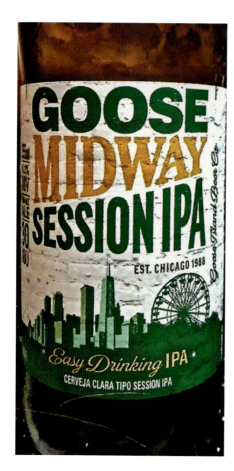

Left: Goose Island's short-lived Midway Session IPA was named after the airport and featured the Chicago skyline and the Navy Pier Ferris wheel. *Courtesy of Goose Island.*

Below: Inspired by the beer and food culture of Belgium, the Hopleaf Bar has been a mecca for craft beer fans with its friendly and elegant Andersonville pub since 1992. *Courtesy of Hopleaf.*

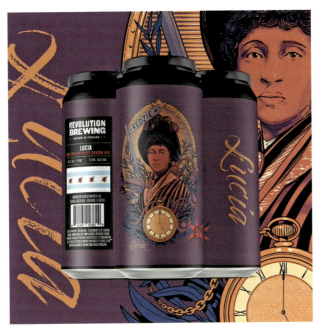

Top: In 2021, Revolution Brewing released as part of its Spirit of Revolt series a dry-hopped spelt saison ale, Lucia, named in honor of labor organizer and anarchist and feminist Lucy Parsons (1853–1942). *Courtesy of Revolution Brewing.*

Bottom: Metropolitan Brewing's mascot of sorts is a robot that evokes Fritz Lang's 1927 German expressionist film classic *Metropolis*. *Photo by author.*

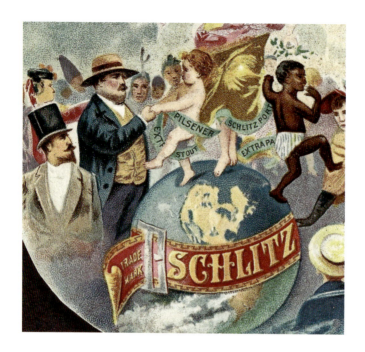

Top: A classic Schlitz ad designed for the 1893 World's Columbian Exposition. *Author collection.*

Bottom: Black door, white wall: the entrance to Moody Tongue at its original Pilsen location. *Photo by author.*

high, sixteen inches around and weighed three pounds, eight ounces when empty; they were four inches deep with a four-and-a-half-inch diameter and could hold one pint, nine ounces.

But the world around Kenna and his partner in crime John "Bathhouse John" Coughlin was rapidly changing. As mobsters such as Jim Colosimo, Johnny Torrio and a young, brash New Yorker named Al Capone began to exert control, the duo's power and influence diminished. Even so, Colosimo and Capone were on good terms with them—Coughlin and Kenna, for example, attended Colosimo's funeral after the gangster was gunned down in his eponymous café, and Capone was a frequent visitor to Kenna's saloon. But Hinky Dink and Bathhouse John's days were clearly numbered.

JIM "BIG JIM" COLOSIMO rose up in the ranks through his vice and racketeering activities in the Levee originally under the watchful eye of Michael Kenna.

Karen Abbott describes Colosimo as a big man "with hulking shoulders and a deliberate, lumbering gait." His "poker face" was "betrayed by his cyclonic personality: He was the kind of man you sensed before you saw."[53] Colosimo was an Italian immigrant from Calabria who controlled the gambling and prostitution rings in Chicago. He trafficked young prostitutes, running a so-called white slavery ring in which young girls were lured from rural areas or small towns with promises of marriage and good jobs but instead were beaten, drugged and raped.

Colosimo had big ambitions. He owned an upscale restaurant called Colosimo's Café at 2126 South Wabash Avenue in the heart of the Levee district, where he played up his Italian heritage with a wall painting of Mount Vesuvius. Colosimo's advertised itself as "Chicago's Oldest Café" or "America's Finest Italian Restaurant." He also emphasized its cultural connections ("Where Bohemia Meets"). Its signature dish was a spaghetti dinner ("One Million Five Hundred Thousand Yards of Spaghetti Always on Hand," declared one menu). It also featured dancing girls. It was the center of high society in Chicago, where politicians, gangsters and celebrities gathered. Regular customers included local and iconic businessmen Potter Palmer and Marshall Field, as well as such visiting entertainers as Al Jolson, George M. Cohan and Enrico Caruso.

Colosimo ruled Chicago's underworld longer than people more famous than him. It was Colosimo who invited Johnny Torrio to leave his native New York to come to Chicago.

Colosimo's was billed as "the finest Italian restaurant in Chicago." It also featured dancing and a "refined" cabaret. *Author collection.*

THE SOFT-SPOKEN TORRIO BECAME Colosimo's right-hand man. He was not your typical gangster. Quiet and restrained, he avoided the limelight, preferring to work behind the scenes. He didn't smoke or drink either. He was a savvy operator known for his excellent organizational skills and had a knack for business. In another time or place, he might have made a strong CEO. He tried to keep the peace between the city's rival gangs.

The plan was for Torrio and his fellow bootleggers to gain control of the local breweries and install "well-paid flunkies" as brewery presidents and plant managers. If the breweries were raided, they would take the fall and be the scapegoats. According to Skilnik, Torrio and his accomplices owned as many as sixty-five breweries in the Chicagoland area, including the Manhattan, Stege, Gambrinus and Hoffman.[54]

Torrio thought the city was big enough for all the gangs in Chicago to get a piece of the vice action, but he underestimated the sectional temperament of the city. As it turns out, he was barely able to hold together his fragile coalition of bootleggers and racketeers. Among the most troublesome was the Irish American mobster Dion O'Banion. O'Banion not only had a short fuse, but he was also very territorial.

DION O'BANION GREW UP in the Kilgubbin neighborhood on the North Side in what is now Goose Island. (Today, Goose Island is famous for the Goose Island Brewery. The brewery at one time made Kilgubbin Red Ale in homage to the Irish history of the area.)

As a boy, O'Banion sang in the church choir at Holy Name Cathedral (he had a beautiful tenor voice). His religious life was short-lived though. He joined a street gang with friends Earl "Hymie" Weiss, Vincent "The Schemer" Drucci and George "Bugs" Moran and, with the advent of Prohibition, turned to bootlegging. Before long, O'Banion and his mates, called the North Side Gang, controlled the North Side. As a front for his criminal operations, he was the co-owner of a florist shop at Chicago and State, across the street from Holy Name.

Mobsters ran the beer rackets in the city, but there was always tension between North Side and South Side gangs. O'Banion had a well-deserved reputation as a violent hothead. Although ostensibly working under Torrio, O'Banion was furious when he perceived that the South Side Italian Genna gang was encroaching on his territory. In response, O'Banion's men stole a truckload of alcohol belonging to the Gennas. Torrio managed to persuade the Genna family not to retaliate, but friction remained not only between O'Banion and Genna but also between O'Banion and Torrio. There was no love lost between the two very different men.

In May 1924, O'Banion unexpectedly announced to Torrio and Torrio's new protégé, Al Capone, who he had brought to Chicago from New York, that he was getting out of the bootlegging business altogether and that he planned to retire and sell his share of the Sieben Brewery that he co-owned with Torrio. Torrio was pleased and just as glad that the troublesome Irishman would soon be out of their way.

O'Banion offered to make a final shipment of real beer to the brewery as a departing gesture of goodwill. Sieben's was licensed for the manufacture of near beer, but in fact real beer was being bottled. O'Banion asked that Torrio accompany him to the brewery one last time to witness the "transaction." But it was a ruse. Torrio didn't know that O'Banion had been tipped that federal Prohibition agents were about to raid the brewery. Because Torrio had prior arrest and conviction records, O'Banion hoped that another arrest would put away the New Yorker long enough so that he, O'Banion, could take over the Chicago bootlegging operations. O'Banion was also arrested, but he got off easy.[55]

Torrio had been double-crossed. It was not something he was about to forget.

On November 10, 1924, three men walked into O'Banion's flower shop. The three gunmen—said to be Frankie Yale, John Scalise and Alberto Anselmi—pumped a series of shots into O'Banion, killing him. The tit-for-tat retaliation continued when associates of O'Banion, Hymie Weiss and Bugs Moran, opened fire on Torrio outside his apartment building. Torrio was severely injured but survived the attack. He was taken to Jackson Park Hospital on the South Side, where his protégé Capone slept on a cot as protection in case someone tried to finish the job. Ultimately, Torrio regained his strength and was fined $5,000 for his activities at the Sieben Brewery and sentenced to nine months in prison in the Lake County Jail in Waukegan, north of Chicago.

The O'Banion assassination sparked a brutal five-year retaliatory gang war culminating in the killing of seven North Side gang members in the St. Valentine's Day Massacre in 1929 (for more on the famous massacre, see page 70).[56]

A Short Respite

During Prohibition, thousands of new licenses were issued to so-called soda parlors. They were supposed to serve only nonalcoholic drinks—hence the name—but in fact, they served real beer. Mayor Bill Thompson knew it. The cops knew it. But virtually everyone turned a blind eye. Ultimately, charges of corruption and the perception that Thompson was losing control of the city led to his downfall. In April 1923, the reform candidate William E. Dever was elected mayor, defeating the incumbent Thompson.

Dever's one term was sandwiched in between Thompson's two terms. Dever was the opposite of Thompson. Unlike Thompson, he refused to maintain the status quo. The city had voted for change, and he would give it change. Thus, for a few short years at least, a mayor who actually took his job seriously and tried to crack down on bootlegging during the so-called beer wars ran Chicago.

Dever's first step was to shut down the illegal breweries in the city. He was determined to root out corruption wherever he found it. Henceforth, shipments of beer would be seized to ensure they obeyed the rule of law. But the breweries were not about to surrender that easily. To get around the law, trucks with near beer were loaded from the front entrances while trucks with real beer were loaded surreptitiously in the back.

A beer war had just begun.

Dever revoked licenses of saloons that sold real beer or whiskey. According to Skilnik, during a two-month period, he revoked the licenses of 4,031 saloons.[57] And he authorized countless brewery raids.

Initially, Dever achieved some success with his law and order campaign and even gained some national and positive media attention. But his well-intentioned attempts were fleeting as gang warfare erupted on the city streets, buoyed by the lawlessness associated with Prohibition, and politicians and police increasingly began to cooperate with the gangs.

Despite Dever's good intentions, Chicagoans were turning impatient. Blood still flowed on the city streets while the beer wars showed no signs of abating. People were also growing weary of Prohibition itself.

Meanwhile, a familiar name was waiting in the wings to rescue the city from the clutches of gang warfare. Thompson was back with promises to reopen every speakeasy in town that Dever had closed. He would, he famously announced, be "wetter than the middle of the Atlantic Ocean." Thompson's promise apparently piqued the interest of the city's bootleggers and gangsters; some even contributed to his reelection campaign. Capone "secretly" contributed $260,000, but according to Bob Skilnik, it was less a contribution than a payoff.[58]

In 1927, Thompson won handily. Chicagoans had not only rejected Dever's well-meaning benevolence but had cast off Prohibition altogether. Dever was so repulsed by the result that he didn't even attend Thompson's public swearing-in ceremony.[59]

Meanwhile, Capone was not only taking over Torrio's various beer territories but was also increasing his power. But there was another figure in town, another do-gooder with an oversize personality and just as strong a knack of garnering publicity as Scarface himself. In 1928, Eliot Ness joined the Chicago branch of the national Prohibition Bureau. Ness had originally made his mark in suburban Chicago Heights before he was ordered to move his operations in Chicago the following year. He had a staff of three hundred agents under his command.

Ness's headquarters was located on the third floor of the Transportation Building in Printers Row and later at the Customs House at 610 South Canal Street. He famously led a team of officers called the Untouchables. A graduate of the University of Chicago, he was twenty-six when, in 1929, he was hired as a special agent of the Department of Justice to head the Prohibition Bureau in Chicago. His task? To investigate and bring Al Capone to justice. Ness also became famous for conducting brewery raids. Fans of popular culture of a certain age know Ness from the television series *The Untouchables* starring Robert Stack, which ran from 1959 to 1963, and later, the 1987 movie starring Kevin Costner as Ness and Sean Connery as a fictional character, an Irish American Chicago cop (despite Connery's Scots burr) who shows the newcomer Ness how to fight back "the Chicago way."

The Transportation Building in Printers Row, the former headquarters of "Untouchable" Eliot Ness. *Photo by author.*

THE MEDIA LOVED AL Capone. He made for good copy. "Public service is my motto," said Capone. He cultivated the press. He loved publicity. He gave them, after all, what they wanted: a good story. "In the brief period he ran Chicago, gunfights and bombings were almost as dependable as sunrises," writes Okrent.[60]

Capone went by many monikers—the Big Fellow to the press, for example—but to most of the world, he was known as Scarface. He began his career in Chicago by running the Four Deuces at 2222 South Wabash Avenue, a four-story building that housed his office and a brothel upstairs in addition to the club below.

Actually, the local newspapers made celebrities out of both Capone and Ness. But the nonstop violence gave Chicago a bad reputation.

The 1929 St. Valentine's Day Massacre changed everything when seven men were murdered at a garage at 2122 North Clark Street in the Lincoln Park neighborhood. Two of the gunmen were wearing police uniforms. The victims included members of Bugs Moran's North Side gang. Capone was assumed to be the mastermind behind it, although he was never charged. Even so, the ferocity of the violence led to uproar and a call to end the bloodshed.[61]

Ultimately, Capone was indicted on June 5, 1931, on charges of tax evasion. He served six years in prison. After his release, he moved to Florida, where he died from syphilis in 1947. In 1931, Thompson was booted out of office yet again, defeated by the wet advocate Anton Cermak. (Bill Thompson was the last Republican to be elected mayor of Chicago.)

Speak Softly and Low

The origin of the word "speakeasy" is debatable. Okrent suggests a possible explanation was that staff asked customers to speak softly in order to avoid attracting attention.[62] It went by other names too: blind pig, blind tiger. Either way, a speakeasy was an illicit bar or establishment that sold alcohol beverages during the Prohibition era. By 1930, the speakeasy was part of American mainstream culture. But despite its ubiquity, or perhaps because of it, drinking in speakeasies could be risky, even poisonous. Yes, there was always a chance that a speakeasy could be raided, but the greatest danger was from the booze itself. "Speakeasy liquor could have been anything from single-malt Scotch smuggled by way of Nassau to diluted embalming fluid."[63]

Speakeasies affected mainstream culture in a profound way. For one, speakeasies democratized public drinking in America. Perhaps the most obvious example of this was the change in the drinking habits of women. Women were a noticeable presence in speakeasies, frequenting bars and clubs and being part of the celebration like their male counterparts, illegal though it might have been. This was the era, after all, of bathtub gin and flappers and the New Woman. No longer was it shocking to see young women having a drink. The new forms of entertainment appealed to women too—jazz bands, torch singers or popular dances like the Charleston and the shimmy.[64]

Women drinking in public was a new thing, and not everyone (read: male) appreciated it. Some bars were slow—very slow—to adjust to the changing times. Until 1969, the bar at the Berghoff served men only. That changed when Gloria Steinem and several other members of the National Organization for Women (NOW) went to the bar and demanded to be served (women were only allowed to eat in the dining room). Steinem's crusade worked, and the era of the male-only bar ended.[65]

Green Door Tavern at 678 North Orleans Street. Established in 1921, the Green Door is housed in a two-story wooden structure that was erected after the Great Chicago Fire but before the fire code ordinance that prohibited the construction of wooden commercial buildings in the central business district. *Photo by author.*

A History of Brewing, Public Drinking and the Corner Bar

By some accounts, there were as many as twenty thousand speakeasies in Chicago by the mid-1920s. After Prohibition ended, many were transformed into nonalcoholic businesses such as drugstores or soda fountains. But some lingered longer than others. Quite a few taverns that are still around today, or that closed fairly recently, were former speakeasies, or so they say. But as Chicago historian Richard Lindberg notes, just because they claim to be does not necessarily mean they were speakeasies.[66]

Former speakeasies that are still open include Marge's Still (established 1885) in Old Town; Green Mill (established 1907), one of the premier jazz clubs in the city; Twin Anchors (established 1910) in Old Town; and Harry Carey's in River North. The latter building was later owned by one of Capone's henchmen, Frank Nitti. Others include the Hideout in Bucktown, Inner Town Pub in Ukrainian Village, the Rainbo Club in Ukrainian Village, the Green Door Tavern in River North and Simon's Tavern in Andersonville.

Prohibition Ends

The repeal of Prohibition took effect in Chicago on December 5, 1933, with the ratification of the Twenty-First Amendment. Due to price competition and consolidation, only those breweries that had sufficient capital to modernize their equipment survived. "Brand loyalty to Chicago's breweries practically disappeared as national breweries with deep pockets advertised heavily," observes Bob Skilnik.

The long-running Tommy Gun's Garage, now closed, turned the Prohibition era into lighthearted entertainment. An interactive musical comedy revue/dinner theater at 2114 South Wabash Avenue (formerly at 1237 South State Street), it featured gangsters, flappers and machine guns and portraits of Al Capone in a brothel-like setting. But it couldn't compete with the pandemic. Before it shut down though, the venue did manage to pull off one last trick: its thirty-first-anniversary reenactment of the St. Valentine's Day Massacre.[67]

Prohibition may be long over, but in recent years, a new tradition has emerged: Dry January, which began in 2013, spurred on by a thriving interest in health and wellness. There is also a trend toward so-called sober bars that pour adult drinks sans the alcohol. In 2020, during the height of the coronavirus pandemic, alcohol consumption fell 5 percent in the United States, Germany, Japan and Brazil, while consumption of low- and no-alcohol drinks rose 1 percent.[68]

Chicago Tribune beer writer Josh Noel notes another reason why nonalcoholic drinks are rising in popularity: they got "interesting" and "innovative," appearing in different forms, including brown ales, wheat ales, pale ales, India pale ales, coffee stouts and pumpkin beers—that is, beers that are the foundation of the craft beer movement.[69]

On the other hand, during the last decade or so, the city has seen a spike in the number of neo-speakeasies/cocktail lounges where the creation of craft cocktails has become its own form of entertainment as patrons watch the theater of mixing drinks at places such as the Violet Hour, Mordecai or Lazy Bird.

Even the bartenders have spawned their own following, including such mixologists as Liz Pierce, Paul McGee and Lee Zaremba. As Zaremba told *Chicago Tribune* food and drink reporter Grace Wong, "How the drink starts isn't the same as the finish. The journey is what I look for."[70]

Chapter 4

THE CRAFT BEER REVIVAL

Goose Island and Beyond

When Peter Hand Brewing closed in 1978, it was the last major brewing company in Chicago until the arrival of craft beer giant Goose Island. But its history dates back to the early 1890s. In 1891, Hand, a Prussian immigrant, opened his own brewery at North and Sheffield Avenues. He called his flagship beer Meister Brau, or Master Brew. To say it was a great success is an understatement.

Hand, though, didn't have much time to enjoy his good fortune, since he died a few short years later in 1899. Aside from shutting down from 1920 to 1933 during Prohibition, his namesake brewery went on, employing hundreds of people until it was purchased by a group of investors and renamed Meister Brau. The investors also expanded operations and launched an aggressive advertising campaign, especially on sports radio. White Sox, Blackhawks and Bulls broadcasts were studded with Meister Brau commercials. In the 1960s and into the 1970s, the brewery sponsored local Blackhawk hockey games and Bulls basketball games over WGN radio, forging an emotional connection between local beer drinkers and their sports teams.[71] Thanks also to a successful regional marketing campaign, Chicagoans began to look at Meister Brau as their local beer.[72]

For a time, things were looking good. Meister Brau even became one of the top breweries in the United States.

But the company overextended itself and began hemorrhaging money. Due to heavy debt and mismanagement, most of its brands were sold to Miller, which repackaged Meister Brau Lite as Miller Lite. In 1973, Peter Hand filed for bankruptcy, and the Meister Brau plant was placed on the auction block when Fred Huber of the Monroe, Wisconsin–based Huber Brewing Company purchased it.

Eventually, new beer brands were released under the Peter Hand label, including Old Chicago. In 1973, the company declared bankruptcy. Five years later, it shut down altogether.

IN THE YEARS AFTER World War II and into the early 1950s, most of the Chicago brewers were family-run operations with little need, or urge, to expand beyond local boundaries. But conditions began to change. During the Prohibition era, Chicago brewers operated under the protection of Capone and company, sharing in the illicit spoils that the mobsters provided them. Without their support, the local brewing industry, notes Bob Skilnik, was reduced "to a handful of small, debt-ridden family businesses." Unable to compete with the bigger breweries, the local brewers began to "crumble."[73]

In an effort to survive, local breweries such as Atlas Brewing Company, Monarch Brewing Company or Birk Brewing Company promoted the idea of brand loyalty and local civic pride with their advertising campaigns. Others such as Schoenhofen's Edelweiss brand preferred a niche approach, as they attempted to cater to a more upscale and discriminating market. Beer advertising reflects this local identity and aspirational urge.

In truth, vintage beer ads ran the gamut from sexist and racist to inventive and imaginative. Atlas Brewing Co. featured a tawny lion with piercing eyes under the header of "King of Tonics." Schoenhofen's Edelweiss beer's "A Case of Good Judgement" ad played up elegance and good taste with an image of an elegantly dressed couple—he in tails and top hat, she in an evening gown. Some ads were clearly xenophobic, especially during the anti-German era of the world wars. McAvoy's Malt Marrow ad, for example, proudly emphasized that its product was "NOT" made in Germany. Others were political in nature, as in 1884, when Conrad Seipp ran an ad during the contentious presidential campaign between Grover Cleveland and James Blaine. And at a time when Americans were concerned over food and drink that might be adulterated—that is, contaminated—and that alcoholic content be accurately labeled, Conrad Seipp boasted that its beer

Top: "A Case of Good Judgement." Schoenhofen Brewery's Edelweiss expects nothing but the best from its customers. *Author collection.*

Bottom: "We may differ in Politics but We all agree that Conrad Seipp's beer is the best." Conrad Seipp's political ad appears to be a reference to the contentious 1884 presidential campaign between the Democrat Grover Cleveland (*left*) of New York and Republican James Blaine (*right*) of Maine. Amidst the turmoil, the well-dressed, waist-coated bartender hovers above it all. *Author collection.*

met "every requirement of the Pure Food Laws" and even featured a smiling figure of Uncle Sam granting his approval with his signature. (The Pure Food and Drug Act—the precursor to the Food and Drug Administration—was passed in 1906.) But some breweries went a step further. For a few short years in the 1930s, Schlitz debuted its so-called Sunshine Vitamin D beer, claiming that brewer's yeast contained vitamin D. In other words, Schlitz's beer was not only tasty; it was also good for you, providing the benefits of the summer sun: sunshine in a glass.

The demise of Peter Hand reflected the brewing industry at the time. Changing business conditions and the changing tastes of consumers led to a preference for national brands over local brands. This was also a time when consumers preferred blander and lighter-tasting beers (beer historians are still mystified by this trend). Mass advertising by national beers only accentuated the shift that their national beers were somehow better in quality than the local brands. Thus, as Bob Skilnik notes, local beers gained a negative reputation as having a "cheap beer" image.[74]

Consolidation and merging of breweries was another major issue. The South Bend–based Drewry's Ltd. bought Atlas and Schoenhofen-Brewery in the early 1950s. The Peter Fox Brewing Company's Chicago plant closed in 1955 and consolidated with the Fox Head Brewery in Waukesha, Wisconsin.[75]

What's more, homogeneous trends and shifting tastes took their toll on local breweries as both Milwaukee and St. Louis brands continued to flex their outsize muscles. More and more Chicago breweries closed or continued to consolidate. A few managed to hold on—but barely.

Before Peter Hand shut down operations, there were a few other breweries in town, including the Chicago Brewing Co., Millrose Brewing, Golden Prairie, Pavichevich Brewing and, most famously, Sieben's. The Chicago Brewing had some luck with Big Shoulders Porter, while Pavichevich had a hit with its Baderbrau pilsner. (A member of former president George H.W. Bush's administration even ordered a case of the brew for the president's suite at the Hyatt Regency during a presidential visit to Chicago in the summer of 1990.)[76] Located on the edge of the South Loop and Bronzeville neighborhoods, Moody Tongue has taken over the building that once housed Baderbrau.

Anheuser-Busch became one of the nation's largest and most successful breweries and exerted its power. Everybody seemed to be drinking the same brand from coast to coast. There was very little room for experimentation. In post–World War II America, the vast majority of midwestern beer drinkers consumed such brands as Budweiser, Miller, Schlitz, Hamms and Blatz. Old Style, in particular, was a Chicago staple. Actually, before Goose Island claimed the title, Old Style at one point called itself Chicago's beer. The ubiquitous signs that still dot the landscape are evidence of the powerful hold it once had.

How Old Style became "Chicago's beer" is an interesting story all its own. Founded by two German immigrants, Gottlieb Heileman and John Gund, the G. Heileman Brewing Company started making Old Style in La

> ### The Original Brewpub
>
> A brewpub is a pub where beer is brewed and consumed on site. Chicago's first microbrewery, or brewpub, was the reinvented Sieben's brewpub, which opened in 1986. Sieben's River North Brewery was located on the 400 block of West Ontario Street and produced four kinds of beer: a German-style lager, a Canadian-style golden ale, an English bitter and a stout. The original Sieben's Brewery closed in 1967. Founded by a German immigrant, Michael Sieben, it moved to 1470 North Larrabee Street in 1876. In 1924, it was the scene of a police raid that resulted in the arrests of Johnny Torrio and Dion O'Banion.
>
> Bob Skilnik, though, maintains that Chicago's first brewpub was far older. In fact, it dates back to 1857, when saloonkeeper John Hoerber raised his saloon, store and boardinghouse and installed a small brewery underneath, "pumping fresh beer to his customers."* Why? Because that year the city council ordered all properties to be raised to a height that would ensure proper drainage.
>
> ---
> * Skilnik, "Building Chicago Was Thirsty Work."

Crosse, Wisconsin, in 1902, but it didn't become available in Chicago until much later, in the 1930s. Lighter-tasting beers were gaining in popularity, and Chicagoans took a liking to the upstart brewery. For a time, it was even brewed in Chicago until it moved back across the border. Once Old Style started sponsoring Chicago Cubs baseball games, that's when its popularity in the city soared. The Old Style signs came later—in the 1970s, when the brewery began giving them away to bars as free advertisement, much like the tied houses of old supplied signage to the old-time saloons. In 2014, rival Anheuser-Busch became the Cubs' official sponsor, but the Old Style signs are still scattered around town.

But when all was said and done, Budweiser was the king of them all—sales-wise at least—with Miller trailing not that far behind. The two rivals fought each other night and day in television ads, especially with the introduction of their lighter brands, Bud Light and Miller Lite, respectively.

Their campaign was successful, but the loser was the American consumer or at least anyone who liked flavor or character in their beer. In 1950, the nation's top-ten brewers made 38 percent of the beer. By 1980, it was more than 90 percent, with Bud and Miller leading the pack.

Local beer drinkers' taste began evolving during the mid-1970s through the 1980s. According to beer historians, the change was partly due to globalization, as more and more Americans became aware that there was a great wide world out there consisting of all kinds of beer of varying taste just waiting to be drunk—beers that were tastier than what they were drinking at their corner bar. More and more people wanted something different, and they were willing to pay a bit more to taste it.

In 1990, a year after the Peter Hand Brewery closed, the Chicago Brewing Company opened in a former pickle factory near the Kennedy Expressway. It was the only commercial bottling brewery in the city at the time. Its flagship brand was called Legacy Lager, but for various reasons—some cite lack of financial funding, amateurish packaging, product contamination and bad beer—the venture failed. (The brewery also made Legacy Red Ale, Heartland Weiss and Big Shoulders Porter.) But the brews never did develop a following in the city. They seemed to lack a certain something—call it buzz, sparkle, momentum. Either way, it failed to capture the imagination, or the taste buds, of the Chicago beer drinker.

But waiting in the wings was another brewery that within a short few years would take the Chicago beer market by storm. It was a craft brewery, and its name was Goose Island.

Goose Island

Before it was bought by Anheuser-Busch in 2011, Goose Island was Chicago's oldest craft brewery, and it remains one of the world's best-known craft beer brands even if many people no longer consider it a craft beer.

It all started with the dream of one man: John Hall. In 1986, Hall was a salesman for a box manufacturer in Chicago. He was middle aged and felt stuck, spinning his wheels at a job that had grown stale. One day, while bored and confined to a plane on a Dallas runway, he began sifting through a flight magazine and read about a tiny brewery in northern California that was run by a trio of friends with a love of beer and experience with homebrewing. They thought their booze might just be good enough to reach an audience beyond their front door. They opened California's first brewpub, Hopland, and the second in the United States since Prohibition.

Their story appealed to Hall. He had always loved beer, and he thought he knew what a good beer tasted like, or should taste like. In particular, he had a special fondness for English bitters, Belgian ales and German lagers, drinks he had quaffed on his overseas travels. American beers paled by comparison.

Before John Hall could try out his dream of creating quality beer in Chicago, he needed a name.

Goose Island is a 160-acre artificial island formed by the north branch of the Chicago River on the west and the North Branch canal on the east and located near North Avenue and Division Street. It is nearly one and a half miles long and a mere half mile across. In the nineteenth century, it was known as Kilgubbin, an Irish enclave of poor immigrants with a reputation for rowdiness and general disorder. Later, it became industrialized with coal plants, grain elevators and a rail yard. At one point, the Sara Lee Corporation, maker of frozen and packaged foods, and Kendall College, the hospitality and culinary arts institution, were located here.

Goose Island merchandise with an emphasis on the goose. *Photo by author.*

There was something about its name, and its gritty past, that appealed to Hall.

Unlike other breweries that moved too fast and expanded before they were ready, Goose Island started out small: in 1988, Goose Island opened as a brewpub in the former Turtle Wax factory at 1800 North Clybourn Avenue. Hall was patient. He allowed Goose Island to establish its reputation before opening a full-fledged brewery at 1800 West Fulton Street, slowly evolving from a microbrewery to a regional brewery. In this way, he methodically built a loyal following while also expanding the market beyond Chicago's city limits.

The fate of Honker's Ale is an example of changing tastes. When Goose Island renovated the original Clybourn location and built a taproom at the Fulton Street production brewery, it dropped its Honker's Ale for national

From Honker's to Sofie

Through the years, Goose Island manufactured several iconic beers: 312 Urban Wheat Ale; Matilda, a critically acclaimed Belgian pale ale inspired by Trappist ales and fermented with the wild yeast Brettanomyces; Sofie, a Belgian-style farmhouse ale, saison; and Bourbon County Stout (now called Bourbon County Brand Stout), an American imperial stout, aged in bourbon barrels from a variety of whiskey distilleries.

Many of Goose Island's past and present beers boasted their Chicago connection: Green Line Pale Ale, in honor of one of the Chicago Transit Authority (CTA) subway lines; Four Star Pils, inspired by the Chicago flag; and the short-lived Midway Session IPA, named after the airport and featuring the Chicago skyline and the Navy Pier Ferris wheel. Two beers in particular played up their Goose Island heritage. The former flagship beer, Honker's Ale, may have been inspired by English country pubs, but it was also a nod to the geese that once flocked to Goose Island. Brewed with roast barley and chocolate malts and made in the Irish tradition, the ruby-colored Kilgubbin Red Ale was named after the original Irish settlement (the label even was decorated with a shamrock).

and local distribution, although it is still available only on draft at its two Chicago taprooms. It was for a time, as Josh Noel notes, "the soul of Goose Island." And for a time, its presence was ubiquitous: on billboards, promoted at festivals and on the radio. But it had fallen out of style and was discontinued.

IN 2011, ANHEUSER-BUSCH BOUGHT Goose Island for $38.8 million in a move that flummoxed the craft beer industry—it seemed like such an odd match.[77]

As of this writing, the Goose Island taproom is still on Clybourn—although a decidedly spruced-over version of its grittier self. After a ten-month renovation, the taproom reopened in 2017 as Goose Island Brewhouse. There are now Goose Island brewpubs in Philadelphia, London, Toronto, Seoul, Shanghai, São Paulo and Monterrey, a growth spurt that was inconceivable until Goose Island was sold to craft beer arch rival Anheuser-Busch InBev. Now it is known and sold around the world and is one of the biggest—if not the biggest—craft beer brands anywhere.

Goose Island is still full of paradoxes. It continues to bill itself as being Chicago's beer, but its most popular brands are made by Anheuser-Busch elsewhere: in Baldwinsville, New York; Fort Collins, Colorado; and Merrimack, New Hampshire. A few beers though, such as Green Line, are still made in Chicago, at the Fulton Street brewery, as well as Sox Golden Ale, brewed for and in collaboration with the city's South Side baseball team.

In 2018, according to the Brewers Association, Chicago was the craft brewery capital of the United States, followed by Denver, Seattle and San Diego. The association also reported that craft beer represented about 12 percent of the overall beer market nationally, with retail sales in 2017 of $26 billion.[78] That's a lot of money, and a lot of beer.

In fact, the craft beer industry is maturing, with most of the growth coming from these smaller microbreweries and brewpubs, industry experts say. Others are diversifying by turning to spirits, especially the larger and long-established breweries.

What is craft beer? In previous incarnations, it might have gone by other names: boutique brewing, cottage brewery, microbrewery, nanobrewery. But *craft beer* sums it up best, and so it stuck.

But what determines craft beer? The size of the brewery? The number of employees? The amount of beer produced annually? According to the Brewers Association and other sources, a brewery can be considered a craft brewery if it subscribes to the following guidelines:

- Small: Annual production of six million barrels of beer or less (approximately 3 percent of U.S. annual sales).
- Independent: Less than 25 percent of the craft brewery is owned or controlled by a beverage alcohol industry member that is not itself a craft brewer.
- Traditional: Beer made by traditional methods with adjuncts that enhance rather than lighten flavor.

The Art of the Beer Label

You can't always judge a beer by its label, but you just might get a sense of the aesthetics behind the company. A brewery's beer label oftentimes makes a statement or at the very least helps the brewery stand out in the crowd—or on the crowded beer shelf. Beer labels also help differentiate themselves from the pack and help to build brand recognition.

Beer label art doesn't receive nearly the recognition it deserves, which is a shame since the art is often inventive, creative and just plain fun.

Among the best and most original artists designing beer labels is Dan Grzeca, a printmaker at Ground Up Press in Chicago who has been making posters and prints for more than twenty years. His work has strong echoes of Mexican art, especially Day of the Dead imagery, as well as echoes of Jasper Johns and Edward Gorey. Grzeca is known for his music posters for such groups and singers as the Black Keys, the Talking Heads, Alabama Shakes, the Lone Bellow, Edward Sharpe and the Magnetic Zeroes, the Lumineers, the Handsome Family, Ray Lamontagne and Chicago-area indie singer-songwriter, multi-instrumentalist and whistler extraordinaire Andrew Bird.

Grzeca frequently works with local craft brewer Hop Butcher for the World (and, before it shut down, Three Floyds in Munster, Indiana—he designed the Dark Lord Day posters), and he often incorporates details from Chicago history into his fantastical designs. His Bughouse Square double India pale ale label, for example, features a one-eyed figure wearing a top hat standing atop a soapbox and carrying a "Power to the People!" sign superimposed over an image of the actual Bughouse Square, the nickname for Washington Square Park. "Bughouse" was slang for a mental health institution. From the 1910s to the mid-1960s, Bughouse Square was the most celebrated, and infamous, outdoor site for free speech in the United States. Each July, the Newberry Library sponsors free-speech gatherings in conjunction with its annual book sale in the park.

The Sands American Pale Ale label is a dark homage to one of the early red-light districts in what is now the upscale Streeterville neighborhood. It features a dagger, a skull, a pistol and a portrait of Cap Streeter, the eccentric local for whom Streeterville is named. (see page 40 for an image of the Sands poster).

A History of Brewing, Public Drinking and the Corner Bar

Bughouse Square citra, mosaic, Simcoe and Nelson sauvin-hopped Double India Pale Ale. Dan Grzeca's beer label for Hop Butcher for the World's double IPA is an homage to Chicago's historic free speech corner, Bughouse Square, located across from the Newberry Library. *Courtesy of Hop Butcher for the World.*

Grzeca's Destination Moon double IPA was named *USA Today*'s Top 10 Best 2016 Beer Labels. The artwork was inspired by the stylized poster of Georges Méliés's 1902 French silent film classic, *A Trip to the Moon*, with its iconic image of a cannon-propelled capsule landing with a giant splat and stuck in the eye of the Man in the Moon.

Chicago artist, actor, one-time bartender and all-around raconteur Tony Fitzpatrick has designed several beer labels for Forbidden Fruit—which bills itself as Chicago's first botanic brewery—and all in his weirdly inimical style reminiscent of comic books, horror films and tattoos. On the brewery website, Fitzgerald explains that his labels are "all a meditation on my childhood." Each label is accompanied by a brief story that appears adjacent to the image.

In 2021, Revolution Brewing released as part of its Spirit of Revolt series its dry-hopped spelt saison ale Lucia in honor of labor organizer and anarchist and feminist Lucy Parsons. Parsons and her husband, Albert Parsons, advocated for an eight-hour workday, among many other causes. In 2017, the stretch of Kedzie Avenue in front of Revolution was named Lucy Gonzalez Parsons Way. The proceeds from sales of the beer benefited Connections for Abused Women and Their Children (CAWC).

Arguably the most playful labels belong to Off Color Brewing in Lincoln Park. Illustrator Nikki Jarecki and graphic designer Tim Breen's whimsical and tongue-in-cheek work features a lion (on Apex Predator's Belgian-style saison) and, best of all, a farmhouse

"Beer for Pizza." Nikki Jarecki's adorably goofy beer label for Off Color Brewing's malt beer is inspired by pizza and soft drink parties. Beer for Pizza is a malt beer that features sweet crystal malts, Belgian dark candy syrup and vanilla with lime juice and citric acid. Fun factoid: Beer for Pizza's "secret ingredient" is kola nut as its source for its mild caffeine kick. *Courtesy of Off Color Brewing. Illustration by Nikki Jarecki. Designed by Tom Breen.*

mouse aptly named Mischief, who also serves as the brewery's mascot of sorts.

"We play with this childlike, playful, fun [style] like children's book illustrations, but they have this edgy twist," Jarecki told the *Tribune*'s Aine Dougherty.[*] Check out their usually but not always black-and-white labels—one color label depicts two mice reading—and you can see little Mischief knitting socks, playing golf, swinging a baseball bat, eating pizza or any other number of improbable activities. Of course, Off Color's taproom is called the Mousetrap.

English-born artist Paul Nudd has created some of the funky labels for Marz Community Brewing, including its black Berliner Weiss with cherries, Bubbly Kriek.

---

[*] Aine Dougherty, "The Art of Beer: Chicago Artists Bring Flair to Local Breweries' Designs," *Chicago Tribune*, February 20, 2019.

Stronger Together: Collaboration and Community

The hallmark of craft beer and craft breweries is innovation *and* cooperation. Craft brewers are renowned for their involvement in their communities through philanthropy, charity donations, volunteerism and sponsorship of local and neighborhood events. People tend to identify with their local craft breweries. Craft breweries and craft pubs form an important fabric of the neighborhood and community life.

Craft breweries often work together as partners rather than rivals. Begyle Brewing and Dovetail Brewery in Ravenswood once teamed up for an Oktoberfestiversary, as they call it, which included special tastings of their respective beers along with food pairings from neighborhood food trucks. Other brewers collaborate on the actual brewing process. In late 2018, three Chicago-area craft breweries—Solemn Oath, Hop Butcher for the World and Miskatonic—collaborated on a special new release: an imperial milk stout made with, and named after, the Hobson oak tree in Naperville, Illinois. The Hobson bur oak tree stood near the intersection of Hobson Road and Greene Road in that west suburban Chicago town for 250 years before it was cut down in 2016 because of decay. A portion of the proceeds went to the Naperville Parks Foundation. In addition, in 2021 Hop Butcher collaborated with Billy Corgan of the Smashing Pumpkins on a beer celebrating the thirtieth anniversary of the rock band's debut album *Gish*.

The founding members of Marz Brewing in Bridgeport have a long running history of arts, activism and socially engaged activities. They are partners and founders of the nonprofit arts organization Public Media Institute, which runs the art space Co-Prosperity Sphere, FM radio station Lumpen Radio and *Lumpen Magazine*. Several of their beers have Chicago-centric names or pay homage to Chicago history. The Machine, an American pale ale, refers to the city's infamously corrupt political organization, and Bubbly Kriek, a Berliner weisse, is a nod to Bubbly Creek, the nickname given to the south branch of the Chicago River. During the early years of the twentieth century, it was known for its pungent aroma: the nearby meatpacking plants dumped their blood and offal into the river. Upton Sinclair's muckracking novel *The Jungle* (1904) brought the area and the unsanitary practices in the American meatpacking industry to the public's attention.

Malört: The Chicago Handshake

Arguably, the most iconic if polarizing drink in Chicago is Jeppson's Malört, a liqueur known for its bitterness and punch (some would even say undrinkability). For better or worse, it has been called Chicago's answer to absinthe. Malört is synonymous with Chicago. For some, it has become a rite of passage. It is especially popular in the Hispanic community. It also forms one-half of the so-called Chicago Handshake, the other half being usually, but not exclusively, Old Style (the beer of choice at Pub Royale in Ukrainian Village is Hamm's).

Malört is the Swedish word for wormwood. In 1934, Swedish immigrant Carl Jeppson created a homemade herbal aperitif that he sold door-to-door and touted for its medicinal purposes, which is the very reason why it was allowed to be sold during Prohibition. Made in Chicago until the mid-1970s, then in Kentucky and finally in Florida, it was acquired by the Pilsen-based CH Distillery in 2018; production returned to Chicago the following year. As its label says, Malört is not for everyone. Jeppson himself referred to it as "two-fisted liquor." The label features an older version of the Chicago flag (three flags instead of the current four). For years, it was only sold in Chicago.

Malört features prominently in Chicago pop culture. It even makes an appearance in Joe Swanberg's 2013 film *Drinking Buddies*, starring Jason Sudeikis, where Sudeikis's character compares it to "taking a bite out of a grapefruit and then drinking a shot of gasoline." The movie is about two co-workers at Revolution Brewery, the real-life Chicago craft brewery; it was set and actually partly shot there. To comedian John Hodgman, Malört tastes like "pencil shavings and heartbreak" (that's meant to be a compliment). Others have compared its taste to sweaty socks, rubber bands and pesticide.

During the early days of the pandemic, CH made Malört hand sanitizer, donating six thousand gallons of it to nonprofits, and in 2020, Revolution teamed up with CH Distillery to create Anti-Hero Malört. It was released in limited amounts during the height of the pandemic, and the companies donated $5,000 each to Comp Tab Relief Fund, which provided aid to hospitality workers.

A History of Brewing, Public Drinking and the Corner Bar

Beyond Goose

In 2018, Chicago had more breweries than any other city in the United States. Some are well known beyond the city limits, others not so much.

Revolution Brewing in Logan Square started as a modest brewpub but now outsells even Goose Island and has become the premier craft beer in the city. In fact, in 2020, Revolution Brewing became Illinois's top-selling craft beer. It has earned the respect of both casual drinkers and hardcore geeks. Hop Butcher for the World started out its brewing life as South Loop Brewing Co. in 2012, but few noticed until they changed their name and rebranded themselves to pay homage to Carl Sandburg's poem "Chicago" and its "hog butcher for the world" line. Each release generates excitement as much for their beers as for the intricate artwork of their beer labels, especially the exquisite work of Dan Grzeca (see sidebar on page 84). Some beers have come to define their individual brewery: Revolution's Anti-Hero or Half Acre's Daisy Cutter.

MANY CRAFT BREWERIES IN Chicago are heavily involved in social justice issues.

When Greenstar, the in-house brewery at Uncommon Ground's coffeehouse, opened in 2014, it was the first all–certified organic brewery in the state of Illinois. Their mission is to "do good beer," which means to make the best beer they can but also to create a "do good beer" program. When patrons come to Uncommon Ground on Clark Street and purchase beer to take home in growlers or howlers, at least 5 percent off the top of each sale goes to a rotating charity of the quarter.

Haymarket Brewing in the West Loop calls itself a bar for "working people—all kinds of working people: first responders, truck drivers, IT technicians, dentists, lawyers, electricians, chefs, brewers.…We celebrate working people in our name, which comes from our location,"[79] Chicago's Haymarket Square, the site of the famous Haymarket Affair of May 4, 1886. That incident—which included a demonstration, riot and bombing—led directly to the creation of the eight-hour workday, and annual May Day celebrations are still held around the globe in its honor.

The Chicago location—Haymarket has a second location in Bridgman, Michigan—has vintage photographs of the events surrounding the Haymarket Affair, including a powerful painting in the front bar area. Several Haymarket beers are named after people associated with the Haymarket Affair, such as Oscar's Pardon, a Belgian-style pale ale after Oscar Neebe, one of the Haymarket Affair men who was found guilty for the murder of police officer Mathias Degan and conspiracy to start a police riot. But Neebe, who always maintained his innocence, was not even present at Haymarket Square on that fateful day. Subsequently, Illinois governor John Peter Altgeld pardoned Neebe in 1893. Another beer, Mathias Imperial IPA, is named in honor of Degan.

The focus of Off Color Brewing in Lincoln Park may be experimental beers, but among their most inspired offerings are beers rooted in history—ancient history. The brewery began in 2013 as a partnership between John Laffler, formerly of Goose Island, and Dave Bleitner, formerly of Two Brothers Brewing. The duo focused on brewing forgotten beer styles, particularly those made in Germany before the Bavarian Purity Law, or Reinheitsgebot, in the fifteenth century.[80] One of particular historic interest is their second collaboration with the Field Museum, Chicago's natural history museum, a beer called Wari.

A team of Field Museum archaeologists led by Dr. Patrick Ryan Williams excavated a site in Peru and discovered evidence of a one-thousand-year-old brewery that existed between AD 600 and 1050. Trace ingredient analysis revealed remnants of maize and molle berries, which showed that the Wari, an indigenous South American people, were making a stronger version of a traditional chicha (corn) beer. Off Color partnered with the Field Museum to re-create "chicha de molle" using ingredients (Peruvian purple corn and pink peppercorns) that are indigenous to Peru. An interesting aside to this historical brew is that they used a very modern ingredient, the light-resistant tetra-hop created by Miller High Life, so that they could put the pink-hued beer into clear bottles.

"As a craft brewery, one of the things that surprises many of our customers is that we brewed a collaboration beer with Miller High Life," Ben Ustick told me. "For years, whenever people asked what our favorite beer was, we'd say High Life. (And not only because they'd send over cases of High Life when we said it.)" Ustick and his team had approached Miller about collaborating together. "Big meets small," he remarked. "Technical acumen and resource meets magic and wishful thinking. Because at the end of the day, we're all brewers. Beer is beer, and it's high time the trope of us versus them is replaced with an understanding of how big and varied the world is."[81]

Revolution has released numerous beers with political, literary or historical themes and/or figures as inspiration: Cross of Gold golden ale was inspired by William Jennings Bryan's famous speech at the 1896 Democratic

> ## Black Brewers and Black Taverns
>
> According to brewing industry data in 2021, African Americans represented about 12 percent of beer drinkers in the United States but a mere 1 percent of brewery owners. The chief reason is the lack of access to capital. On the other hand, one of the premier brewmasters is an African American, Garrett Oliver, of Brooklyn Brewery. He is also the editor of *The Oxford Companion to Beer*.
>
> As of this writing, Charles St. Clair's Black Horizon Brewing in suburban Willow Brook is the only Black-owned brewery in Illinois, although there have been others or at least attempts to open breweries in African American neighborhoods. The African American–owned Vice District Brewing closed its South Loop in 2019, and in 2020, the long-planned Englewood Brews failed to get off the ground.
>
> In September 2020, Black Horizon was one of thirty or so Chicago breweries and more than one thousand worldwide to brew an imperial stout called Black Is Beautiful, an initiative intended to raise funds and public awareness for social and racial injustice.
>
> The only Black-owned LGBTQ bars in Chicago are the Jeffrey Pub in the South Shore neighborhood, which has been serving the Black and Brown LGBTQ communities for nearly sixty years, and Nobody's Darling in Andersonville, which opened in May 2021 and is named in honor of an Alice Walker poem.

National Convention in Chicago; Coffee Eugene, a porter, is named after Eugene Debs, an American union leader and activist who led the Pullman Railroad strike in 1894; Smash the Windows, a nitro milk stout, was brewed with the South Side Irish folk rockers the Tossers; Harpers Ferry brown ale is named after the abolitionist John Brown's raid on Harpers Ferry in 1859; Louie Louie is after the infamous 1963 rock classic; and two takes on Melville's *Moby Dick*, Moby Wit (the Great White Ale) and Queequeg's Coffin, a gin barrel–aged imperial wheat.

Craft Breweries in Post-Pandemic Chicago

The COVID-19 pandemic has had a devastating effect on the Chicago craft beer community, probably the biggest blow to the beer industry since Prohibition. A few have shut down, including Argus Brewery in the Roseland neighborhood and Motor Row Brewing and Vice District in the South Loop. But as some closed, others added a second location, such as Forbidden Root, which moved into the former location of the Michelin-starred brewpub Band of Bohemia in Ravenswood, as well as Ravinia Brewing and Marz Community Brewing, both in Logan Square. Still others opened or announced they were opening up a taproom: Lake Effect in Jefferson Park and Hop Butcher for the World in Logan Square. Orkenoy is a brewpub that opened in the Kimball Arts Center in Humboldt Park. The latter's Nordic name is loosely translated as "desert island" in Norwegian, but to these ears, it evokes the Orkney Islands. It serves Scandinavian-style open-faced sandwiches in its brightly lit, welcoming space. Crushed by Giants, a brewpub off Michigan Avenue, opened right before the pandemic. Moody Tongue Brewing moved from its Pilsen location to the South Loop, on the edge of Bronzeville. In 2021, Moody Tongue, which offers a twelve-course beer pairing, was awarded two stars from Michelin, which makes it the nation's only Michelin-starred brewpub.

Chapter 5
COMMUNITY IN A GLASS

THE CORNER BAR

A good bar is a bouquet of warm memories.
—Dave Hoekstra, journalist

The bartender has command authority.
When you're behind the bar, you own the bar.
—Bill Savage, professor, author and Chicago saloon scholar

Don't bother with churches, government buildings or city squares. If you want to know about a culture, spend a night in its bars.
—Ernest Hemingway

For years, the corner bar was a retreat, a refuge, a gathering place, a place of sanctuary, a home away from home. Sociologist Ray Oldenburg calls it a third place or the "great good place."[82] Bars and restaurants often anchor a neighborhood and function as ballast against rough economic winds. But they also echo and reflect moments—chapters—of our lives: the good and the bad. Or as Oldenburg notes, they get you through the day. To *Chicago Tribune* reporter and columnist Rick Kogan, a great neighborhood tavern can be something as simple as offering a great jukebox, cheap drinks and "no attitude." Kasey's Tavern in Printers Row is an excellent corner bar that happens to be in the middle of a block.

Writers have long been associated with bars and booze. For historic and social reasons, most of them have been male (Hemingway, Fitzgerald, O'Neill, Cheever, Carver), but sometimes women have written about their boozy experiences. I am thinking here of Dawn Powell, Jean Rhys and especially Patricia Highsmith. In 2013, the English essayist and cultural critic Olivia Laing published *The Trip to Echo Spring: On Writers and Drinking*. As she traveled across America, she evocatively explored the often fraught and complicated relationship between alcohol and creativity.

Some bars—both real and fictitious—are known the world over: the White Horse Tavern and McSorley's in New York, Napoleon House and Old Absinthe House in New Orleans, Harry's Bar in Venice, Davy Byrnes' Pub (made famous by James Joyce in *Ulysses*), Samuel Johnson's old haunt Ye Old Cheshire Cheese in London and, going all the way back to Geoffrey Chaucer's time, the Tabard Inn, established in 1307. It was at the Tabard in Chaucer's *The Canterbury Tales* that thirty or so pilgrims met up at the inn in the Southwark district of London before making their famous pilgrimage to the shrine of Thomas Becket in Canterbury. And then there is the titular Cheers, everyone's favorite Boston pub with everyone's favorite bartender, Sam Malone (Ted Danson). The Dickens, named after Charles Dickens, in J.R. Moehringer's memoir *The Tender Bar*, is the epitome of the neighborhood bar where everyone has your back. (In 2021, the book was made into a film starring Ben Affleck and directed by George Clooney.) On the other hand, Harry Hope's saloon and rooming house in Eugene O'Neill's iconic 1946 play *The Iceman Cometh* is populated by alcoholics and prostitutes who drink themselves into oblivion, their lives built on the flimsiest of pipe dreams.

Historically, the bartender has played the starring role at the corner bar, but it's the regulars who typically provide the entertainment. Everybody has a story to tell, even if they don't tell it. The bartender knows this. In an earlier era, he—it was always a man—might have been known as a barkeep. He was friend to all. To his enemies, though, he symbolized decay and chaos, an affront to common decency. Either way, the bartender was part psychologist and part philosopher, part peacemaker and even matchmaker, an expert on everything from daily living to city politics. And if he wasn't an expert, he was always guaranteed to have an opinion. The wisest bartenders, though, knew when to talk and when to keep their mouths shut.

Historic Bars:
From Gore & Chapin to Hannah & Hogg

Not every bar was a neighborhood bar. The high-end taverns tended to be located downtown in the Loop. "The fancier places, fitted like private clubs, had private dining rooms, billiard parlors and barrooms fitted with onyx wainscoting, matched veneers, and uniformed bartenders."[83] Two of the swankiest of these saloons in nineteenth-century Chicago were Chapin & Gore and Hannah & Hogg. Both were distilling and bottling companies that also operated their own saloons.

James J. Gore, a Georgia-born entrepreneur who spent some time out west digging for gold as a forty-niner, and Gardner S. Chapin, a stockbroker, opened their first grocery store at the corner of State and Monroe Streets in 1865 and then added a liquor department. They even released their own brand, which they called 1867 Sour Mash. Before long, they began selling their own whiskey.

During the Chicago Fire, Gore reportedly hired men to roll barrels full of bourbon and rye into Lake Michigan to save it from the flames. The press loved it, and their fame grew. Taking advantage of the whiskey, which they claimed to be as "fine as silk," they sold it for an inflated price under the name of Lake Whiskey.

In post-fire Chicago, they operated a chain of retail branches and sampling rooms. In 1874, they added a restaurant and an upstairs saloon at their Monroe Street location. The saloon had the ambiance of an art gallery, with a grand bar serving whiskeys and other assorted liquors. The saloon became known for its collection of full-size caricatures of contemporary figures, including Mayor Carter Harrison I, President William McKinley, Charles Comiskey, Oscar Wilde and Mark Twain.

After Gore died in 1891, Chapin continued the business until Prohibition forced him to shut down. The brand name of Chapin & Gore, though, was revived after Prohibition was repealed. The Chapin & Gore brand is still available in select markets under the name Chapin & Gore Old Reserve, produced by Heaven Hill Distillery.[84]

Chapin and Gore's chief rivals at the time were Alexander Hannah and David Hogg, two immigrants from Scotland. Hannah was a traveling salesman in the liquor industry, and Hogg was a paperhanger and later a painter. Hogg arrived in Chicago in 1869 and Hannah a few years later

Each Hannah & Hogg outlet featured larger-than-life stone statues situated outside as an advertising draw, such as this statue of the Scots' national bard, Robert Burns, which stood at the 188 West Madison Street location. *Chicago History Museum, iCHi-064207.*

in 1872. Combining forces, they opened a saloon in 1873 called, appropriately enough, the Thistle at 190 Madison Street. It branched out into a wholesale and retail liquor and cigar business, adding other outlets over the years. Each outlet had larger-than-life stone statues situated outside as an advertising draw, such as a statue of the Scots' national bard, Robert Burns, which stood at the 188 West Madison location, or novelist Sir Walter Scott and his loyal dog Maida at 112 Monroe Street.

Hannah and Hogg were liquor dealers who bought whiskey in bulk, bottled it and sold it under their own labels with such names as Home Rule, Old Cameron, Silver Thistle and Ramshead. Eventually, they operated the elegant Brevoort Hotel at 120 West Madison Street and moved their offices there. The Brevoort was famous for many things but perhaps none more than its ornate and stunning bar: a round bar with a glass rail and mirrored columns decorated with tile patterns and a chandelier hanging in the middle. During its heyday, it was the preferred choice of the city's elite.

Hannah retired in 1913 and died the same year. Hogg ran the hotel until 1920. The hotel was demolished after World War II.

ANOTHER POPULAR BUT ALTOGETHER different kind of saloon was Heinegabubeler's on State Street, which was part of a national chain (the first saloon opened during the 1893 World's Columbian Exposition). Part museum, peep show and amusement park, Heinegabubeler's showed early motion pictures. It also housed a gymnasium and reading rooms and roof garden.

Thomas Collier, its owner, intended it to be "a joker's paradise," a saloon that turned silly, juvenile barroom humor into a successful business enterprise—the kind of place where Chicagoans, as the *Tribune* noted, "took their country cousins for entertainment." Collier certainly had a sense of humor, and anyone who entered his emporium had to have one too. Trapdoors, traps, baits, trick furniture—the brass bar rail was actually rubber so when patrons picked up change from the counter they received an electric shock. The "free lunch" buffet consisted of soap that resembled cheese, rubber beets, chopped hay and oats.

First-time visitors were the butt of jokes and gags (they were given mugs with holes in them). Customers who were good sports about it were given free food and drink, while those who complained were shown the door. It was a latter-day version of Dick's Last Resort, the national bar and restaurant chain known for its intentionally obnoxious staff who serve their orders with a heavy dose of sarcasm.

Literary Hangouts

A few historic bars were literary hangouts. Among the most famous was Schlogl's, a dark, smoky German tavern at 37 North Wells Street along so-called Newspaper Row and founded in 1879 by its namesake Joseph Schlogl less than a decade after fire devastated the city. It boasted an ornate tin ceiling, large oil paintings of monks drinking wine in ancient cellars and heavy oak chairs and a cut-glass chandelier. This was during the era when Chicago was a newspaper town with the likes of Ben Hecht and Charles MacArthur of *Front Page* fame trolling the streets. Other literary scribes, poets, columnists and critics came too: Carl Sandburg, Sherwood Anderson, Robert Herrick, Edgar Lee Masters and Maxwell Bodenheim, but also Clarence Darrow, John Gunther, Irwin St. John Tucker, Henry Justin Smith and Samuel Putnam. It is featured prominently in literary critic Harry Hansen's *Midwest Portraits*. Vincent Starrett, the Chicago book critic, compared it, favorably, to London's Mermaid Tavern or Samuel Johnson's favorite haunt, the Mitre Tavern, on Fleet Street. To others, it was Chicago's version of New York's Algonquin Round Table. According to legend, free meals were given on Fridays to journalists—if their bylines appeared in the paper that day.

Schlogl's was also known for its food. If it was a daytime crowd, the choice may have been German apple pancakes "as big as an elephant's ear," as John Drury once described them in his 1931 classic *Dining in Chicago*. In the evening, the tavern's famous hamburger steaks fried in butter were served or the ever-present wiener schnitzel. The menu even promised "owls to order," which was guaranteed to raise a few eyebrows to those who were not in on the joke or familiar with the quirky humor of the owners.

Schlogl's, Chicago's answer to New York's Algonquin Round Table. Here the best of Chicago journalists and authors, many from the *Chicago Daily News*, gathered to celebrate the irrepressible Ben Hecht in 1924. *Seated, left to right*: Philip Davis, lawyer; Alfred MacArthur; Ashton Stevens, *Chicago Herald-American* theater critic; William F. McGee; Charles Collins, *Chicago Tribune* theater critic; Harry Hansen, *Chicago Daily News* reporter and author of *Midwest Portraits: A Book of Memories and Friendships* (1925); Le Roy T. Goble, ad man; John Gunther, journalist and author of *Death Be Not Proud*; Peter Hecht; physician Morris Fishbein; J.U. Nicholson; and Lloyd Lewis, *Chicago Daily News* drama critic and columnist. *Standing, left to right*: Richard Schneider, Schlogl's maître d'hotel; Dwight Haven; Keith Preston, *Chicago Daily News* literary critic and journalist; Pascal Covici, book publisher and editor; Ben Hecht, *Chicago Daily News* reporter and co-writer (with Charles MacArthur) of *The Front Page*; Vincent Starrett, *Chicago Daily News* reporter and author of *Born in a Bookshop: Chapters from the Chicago Renascence* (1965); and Henry Justin Smith, managing editor of the *Chicago Daily News*. *Courtesy Newberry Library.*

Other vintage bars of that era included St. Hubert's Old English Grill, an old-fashioned English inn that was located at 316 South Federal Street in the Union League Club building. According to John Drury, it was the kind of place where "pink-coated English waiters" brought patrons "a mutton chop so thick and juicy that its taste lingers in your mouth for days."[85]

A History of Brewing, Public Drinking and the Corner Bar

SOME LITERARY BARS WERE more modest but just as full of character. Years later and in a different era, O'Rourke's in Old Town was a legendary literary Irish bar famous for its large, oversized black-and-white photographs of Irish writers Sean O'Casey, George Bernard Shaw, James Joyce and Brendan Behan hanging on the walls of its original location on Wells Street. And when it moved a short walk away to 319 West North Avenue, Oscar Wilde, W.B. Yeats and Samuel Beckett joined them. Members of the James Joyce Society met there too. The North Avenue location closed in late 1989 and moved again the following year to 1625 North Halsted Street, down the street from the Royal George Theatre. Two years later, in 1991, Steppenwolf would move across the street. (The pub's wooden bar appeared in Steppenwolf's 2002 production of *The Time of Your Life*. The original O'Rourke's globe was rescued from salvage and put on display at the theater's café and cocktail bar.)

It was a writers' hangout. Journalists, authors, poets—they all came. Many were famous, such as Nelson Algren, Saul Bellow, columnist Mike Royko and author and historian Studs Terkel. There were also police officers, lawyers, teachers, ad people, judges and even construction workers. Actors from Second City, such as John Belushi, and folk singers from the Earl of Old Town, including John Prine and Steve Goodman, dropped in. As former regular Warren Leming said, at O'Rourke's "you [could] always get a good conversation going."

Arguably O'Rourke's most famous regular was the late *Chicago Sun-Times* film critic Roger Ebert. Ebert wrote about it lovingly on his blog. "O'Rourke's was our stage," he confessed, "and we displayed our personas there nightly....From the day it opened on December 30, 1966 until the day I stopped drinking in 1979, I drank there more or less every night." It became his makeshift office, his home away from home. He even began interviewing actors there for his *Sun-Times* articles, including Jack Lemmon, Charlton Heston, Gene Hackman and Cliff Robertson.

O'Rourke's was also the place where Ebert and other regulars watched on television the moon landing or the street protests that erupted after Dr. Martin Luther King Jr. was assassinated. In 1968 during the Days of Rage, anti–Vietnam War protesters demonstrated on the Old Town streets, just outside O'Rourke's doors.

When it moved to Halsted, it attracted a theater crowd, including actor Brian Dennehy when he was in town.

O'Rourke's embraced eccentricity and individualism. People came to drink, smoke (in the days when smoking in bars was legal) and argue.

Chicago Beer

They would break out in song, singing along to the jukebox. Bagpipers reportedly drank free.

O'Rourke's closed in 2001. Jay Kovar, the former bartender who bought the place, cited the changing times for the reason. "The whole drinking scene has changed in Chicago," he lamented.

Bar Lit

Booze and writing have always been big parts of the Chicago literary scene. Bars such as the Hideout, which is also a music venue, have hosted regular readings and/or literary events, as have Danny's Tavern, Weeds and other venues. Since the city was also once known as a big newspaper town, one of the most famous characters happened to be the fictitious barkeep of a working-class saloon in Bridgeport, Finley Peter Dunne's Martin Dooley, the sage and street corner philosopher.

Mr. Dooley spoke in a thick Irish brogue and dispensed his wisdom while offering ample pours to his customers along Archer Avenue in the Bridgeport neighborhood. Dooley, a survivor of the Great Irish Famine, was known for his acerbic commentary on events of the day, especially the behavior of politicians. When he spoke, everyone listened.

Dooley was based on an actual bartender, Jim McGarry, who owned a bar on Dearborn near Madison and was famous in his day for his warmth and wisdom and his gregarious nature. McGarry's bar was a favorite spot for politicians, judges and actors. The rosy-cheeked and dignified McGarry epitomized the nineteenth-century ideal of the bartender. He had an opinion about everything. He attracted people from all works of life, from the powerful to everyday folks. Among the patrons who gravitated to his bar was the young newspaperman Finley Peter Dunne. Dunne loved the ambiance of the bar, but most of all, he loved McGarry's sparkling personality and his gift of gab. Before long, Dooley began writing McGarry's words down and moved the setting of the tavern from downtown to

Martin Dooley was the fictional barkeep of a fictitious Irish tavern on Archer Road or, as he referred to it, "Archey Road." At the peak of his popularity, Dooley's creator Finley Peter Dunne was considered one of the great American humorists of his day, comparable to Mark Twain. *Wikipedia Commons.*

Archer Avenue in Bridgeport, then a predominantly Irish community on the South Side. Martin Dooley became the barkeep of Archer, or Archey Road, and McGarry was transformed into a character named Hinnissey or Hennessey.[86]

The first Mr. Dooley articles appeared when Dunne was chief editorial writer for the *Chicago Post*. In sum, Dunne wrote more than seven hundred Dooley pieces, many of which were published in book form. Most of his essays were humorous and droll commentaries on contemporary life in Chicago as seen through the eyes of a fictional Irish barkeep. Finley Dunne's Tavern in the Lakeview neighborhood honors Dunne's memory and even has a sandwich named after him (Dooley's sandwich consists of grilled cheese with a fried egg and bacon or sausage).

In contrast, James T. Farrell's *Studs Lonigan* depicts the unsavory underbelly of the working-class saloon culture. The characters drink their sorrows away in neighborhood bars. Their only respite from life is the bottle. Studs and his friends use alcohol as an escape from boredom and the misery of their confined lives.

Sometimes particular writers are associated with particular bars: Joseph Mitchell and McSorley's Old Ale House in New York's East Village or Eugene O'Neill and the Golden Swan in Greenwich Village. The literary barfly Charles Bukowski will be forever linked to Los Angeles and its seedy bars. The connection between Nelson Algren and Chicago is also strong. Few writers knew their way around a bar as well as Algren. He was a regular at taverns throughout Wicker Park and nearby neighborhoods.

Algren's *The Neon Wilderness*, a short story collection published in 1947, featured a cast of petty criminals, card sharks, junkies, hookers, hustlers and assorted misfits. In stories such as "A Bottle of Milk for Mother," "The Face on the Barroom Floor," "Design for Departure," "Katz," "Stickman's Laughter" and "How the Devil Came Down Division Street," he wrote about the drunks, barflies and various misfits who inhabited the area around Milwaukee and Division populated by dive bars, rooming houses and cheap hotels. According to Dominic Pacyga, some sixty taverns lined Division Street at one time, and most offered live music.[87]

Algren lived in an apartment at 1523 West Wabansia Avenue—it was there that he carried on his torrid love affair with the French feminist Simone de Beauvoir—and later in a third-floor apartment at 1958 West Evergreen Street.[88]

Nelson Algren's *The Neon Wilderness* (1947). The twenty-four stories here, including "How the Devil Came Down Division Street," "A Bottle of Milk for Mother" and "The Face on the Barroom Floor," are mostly set in the then Polish American "ghetto" of Wicker Park. *Author collection.*

Frankie Machine, the protagonist of his 1949 novel *The Man with the Golden Arm*, lived in the Division Arms Hotel at 1860 West Division Street. On the ground floor was a fictional tavern with the evocative and nautical name Tug & Maul Bar (the Rainbo Club is said to have served as the model for it), operated by Anthony "Antek" Witwicki. It was the kind of place where only whiskey and beer were served. "For Antek held to the old days and the old ways, familiar whisky and well-tried friends," writes Algren. "He'd roll you for the drinks and give you a square shake, friend of passing stranger, every time." *The Man with the Golden Arm* won the National Book Award for fiction in 1950.[89]

SMALL HOMAGES TO ALGREN continue to pop up in Wicker Park and surrounding neighborhoods.

In 2018, an Algren-inspired bar, the Neon Wilderness, opened at 1270 North Milwaukee Avenue in the heart of the former Polish Broadway, where Division, Milwaukee and Ashland converge. But instead of whiskey and beer, it specialized in "fancy cocktails" and, perhaps in a nod to Algren, cheap beer. The brewpub Piece Brewery and Pizzeria on North Avenue serves Golden Arm Kölsch beer. Down the road a bit in Logan Square, Weegee's Lounge is a low-key place with a 1940s vibe serving classic cocktails and craft beers that is the kind of tavern that Algren would have frequented. It is named in honor of the great New York–based street photographer and photojournalist Weegee (real name: Arthur Fellig), who was known for his unblemished portraits of street people and street scenes. The closest Chicago equivalent to Weegee was arguably the photojournalist Art Shay (1922–2018), who captured the gritty streets of Nelson Algren's Chicago and had a long friendship with him. (To get a sense of what these bars might have looked like circa the 1940s, see the iconic 1948 film noir *Call Northside 777*, starring James Stewart as a dogged, fedora-wearing reporter trying to uncover the killer of a police officer who stopped in for a drink at a mob-owned saloon.)

Shay and Algren met in 1949 when Shay was working as a photojournalist for *Life* magazine. He persuaded the editors to publish a piece on the author. Together, they roamed the city streets, frequenting Algren's favorite haunts, especially around Damen and Division, and thereby cementing their friendship. A famous photograph taken by Shay captures Algren in front of the Polonia Bar, the setting of his 1947 short story "How the Devil Came Down Division Street," a tall tale about the "biggest drunk on Division Street."[90]

A completely different literary landscape was captured in David Mamet's profanity-laced play *Sexual Perversity in Chicago*, which premiered at the Organic Theater in 1974 and is set in Chicago's singles bar scene. It was adapted into a movie, *About Last Night*, twice, in 1986 and 2014. The first adaptation was shot at Mother's on Division Street, where the singles bar was said to be "invented."

Pickled Herrings and Zimne Piwo

For decades, neon signs lured customers into bars. Nowadays, they are not as common as they used to be, but a few still remain. One of the most distinctive bar signs—certainly the goofiest—is Simon's Tavern in Andersonville. It's hard to miss: at night, the blue and yellow colors of the Swedish flag shine brightly as a fish—a "pickled herring"—donning a Viking helmet holds a martini glass in its fin. Inside is just as eccentric. Along with various Viking paraphernalia (statues, helmets, Viking ships), worn couches in the back invite people to stay and perhaps savor, if available, the Swedish glögg, a tasty combination of hot port wine with aquavit and various spices. There's a lovely, ramshackle, well-lived feel that encourages folks to linger.

Simon's also boasts a handsome mural that features deer hunting scenes. The mural was painted by neighborhood resident Sig Olsen. One of the deer hunters is the original owner, Simon Lundberg, and his son, Roy. Lundberg emigrated from Sweden in the early twentieth century. After World War I, he opened a grocery store in Andersonville, but during Prohibition, he was given an offer he couldn't refuse from local bootleggers to sell whiskey with his coffee. After Prohibition ended, Lundberg turned the former grocery store/speakeasy into a bona fide tavern. Like many neighborhood emigrant taverns, Simon's provided basic functions for its patrons. Swedish laborers, for example, cashed their checks here and enjoyed a free buffet on Friday paydays. *Skal*!

Other signs are more prosaic—"Bottles and Cans," "On Draft," "Cold Beer" or the ubiquitous "Package Goods." Sometimes the language is Polish ("Zimne Piwo"), sometimes Spanish ("Cerveza Fria"). Oftentimes bars don't even have a name, just Pabst and Hamm's neon signs in the window.

Cheap Beer and Conversation

Chicago has all kinds of bars and subgenres of bars that often revolve around notions of identity: sports bars, single bars, gay bars, music bars, comedy bars, bars that cater to particular occupations, immigrant bars, cocktail lounges and dive bars. *Dive bar* can a loaded term. Some find it pejorative and even condescending, while others claim it as a badge of honor. (For an often hilarious and sharply observant take on the former perspective, see Bill Savage's "Against Dives: A Rant," which was filmed at the Hopleaf in December 2015 and is available on YouTube.)

But what would we do without dive bars? Dive bars often are the anchors of a neighborhood. In many ways, they are the essence of Ray Oldenburg's "great good place." Dives are more than just a place to have a drink; they become an indelible part of people's lives, as familiar as their own home.

Dive bars can be found anywhere and everywhere, of course. Some have been at the same corner for so long that it appears they have always been there. And some dive bars, such as the Hideout and the Montrose Saloon, offer live music.[91] The *Chicago Tribune*'s Adam Lukach calls Skylark in Pilsen a "true neighborhood" dive bar and compliments its cheap drinks, first-rate food and laidback crowd.

Inner Town Pub (or ITP, for short) in Ukrainian Village is both a classic Chicago corner dive and a classic corner bar. "It's not the most beautiful, but it has an ensnaring charm," writes Michael Nagrant in the *Chicago Tribune*. In its prior life, it was a Polish bar and before that—what else?—a speakeasy. Dimly lit with Christmas bulbs and Tiffany-style stained-glass lamps, it reportedly was a favorite of Gillian Flynn of *Gone Girl* fame when she lived in the neighborhood. In its earlier days, the Smashing Pumpkins were here too. It is known for its unusual décor (a stuffed moose head, a life-size statue of Elvis) as much as for its sea shanty evenings.

"We're a niche business that caters to our local clientele," Inner Town Pub owner Denis Fogarty told the *Tribune*'s Josh Noel.[92] It's the kind of place where you can get a Chicago Handshake for five dollars, play free pool, listen to music or just hang out—the essence of a neighborhood

> ### Irish Sessions: Entering In and Out of Time
>
> Music bars are a special category of their own, but perhaps none is as distinctive and increasingly rare as the Irish pub that features traditional Irish music: Irish sessions. A session is the Irish equivalent of a jam session—a mélange of flutes and fiddles and such—even though it is much more than that. In fact, its main feature is an "endless variety within a fixed framework," as the late Belfast poet Ciaran Carson aptly described it. Irish pubs that presented sessions included the Abbey Pub, the 6511 Club and the Irish Village. The tradition continues at such places as Chief O'Neill's, Mrs. Murphy's Bistro, Galway Arms and Lanigan's Irish Pub, among others.

joint. Their website sums it up: "Come for the free pool, reasonably priced drinks. But stay because of the hospitality. The ITP is here for everyone on good days and bad." Their other mantra is just as important, and in caps no less:

BE KIND
OR LEAVE
THANK YOU

What exactly are dive bars? Many of them just take cash and sell cheap beer. The Levee, a cash-only corner bar at Pulaski and Fullerton on the Northwest Side, has a colorful history: it was the former site of the burlesque club the Gayety Village. Nisei Lounge in Wrigleyville—its name refers to second-generation Japanese immigrants—was founded in the early 1950s when the neighborhood was a Japanese enclave. Now it appeals to a new generation of regulars who appreciate its traditional vibe.

Either way, the term *dive bar* is often used as a term of endearment. "Dive bars," wrote one observer, "are lived in, died in…laughed and cried in a stranger's arms in, at once fully yourself and completely anonymous in. They're where folks go to drink, to lie, to love, to sigh."[93]

Beneath the dive bar on the drinking establishment chain is the taproom, the very antithesis of the corner bar. They're the kind of places where patrons come just to drink—and the more the better. Nobody goes to a taproom to socialize. If the corner bar is the place where everyone knows your name, the taproom is the kind of place where one can wallow in anonymity. Although not as prominent as they once were—in 2003, Mark Anderson claimed that Chicago had more taprooms "than any other city in the country, hands down"—they are still scattered around town, an indelible part of the drinking landscape.

Jimmy's Woodlawn Tap on 55th Street in Hyde Park is a combination dive and neighborhood bar. With its battered mahogany bar, cheap bar food and cash-only policy, it is the epitome of the dive bar. But since it is also essentially the "house bar" of the University of Chicago, it caters to students and professors (there is a small reference library above the bar in a back room, including Encyclopedia Britannica, *Bartlett's Familiar Quotations*, Shakespeare, Norton's poetry anthology and the Bible) and visiting literati. University of Chicago students tended bar here. Regulars over the years have included Saul Bellow and Margaret Mead. When Dylan Thomas was speaking at the university, he stopped by (reportedly three times). The great Irish poet Seamus Heaney came here too.

The "Jimmy" in Jimmy's Place refers to Jimmy Wilson, who ran the bar from 1948 until his death in 1999. Jimmy Wilson loved what he did and was very good at making people feel good. He knew his customers' names, and he never forgot a face. He brought people together. The secret to his success? "Good bartenders and the right location, that's what made this place," he said.

Wilson opened the Tap in the 1950s, when nearly forty bars lined the street. Now Jimmy's is the last man standing.

What also sets Jimmy's apart is its historic mural, informally known as "Moulin Jimmy's." Moulin Jimmy's mural depicts a night at Jimmy's Woodlawn Tap sometime in the mid-1950s. A few of the people are minor celebrities or at least used to be (Andrew Duncan, a founding member of the Compass Players; poet Joffre Stewart), but mostly it's people from the neighborhood or professors at the University of Chicago. It captures the liveliness of the time and the place. People hold up signs ("Wright Is Love." "Mies Is Love." "Danger Army Art Crossing."). A Pete Seeger–like figure strums a guitar, perhaps in a nod to the University of Chicago folk festival. A somber-looking man reads the stock report. One patron looks like Mike Nichols, who was a student at the university. Improv comedy has its roots here: the founders of the Compass Players, a predecessor to Second City and *Saturday Night Live*, drank here. On the other hand, a woman looks at a handheld mirror and sees a skeleton as her reflection.

The artist was Art Castillo, a then-twenty-four-year-old who grew up nearby and later became a regular at Jimmy's. He completed his panoramic mural in 1955.[94]

THE OLD TOWN ALE HOUSE is both dive bar and literary hangout. Eric Van Gelder opened the Ale House in 1958 as a hangout for writers, journalists, artists and performers from the nearby Second City. Van Gelder is the same gentleman, and nautical aficionado, who owned the great and lamented John Barleycorn Memorial Pub, which was, according to Sean Parnell, John Dillinger's favorite pub. The world, and neighborhood, around it may have changed, but the Ale House remains essentially the same. For years, it was owned by Arthur and Beatrice Klug. When Arthur died in 2005, Beatrice asked longtime friend and regular Bruce Elliott and his wife, Tobin Mitchell, to take over, but with one caveat: that they change as little as possible. That was fine with Elliott since it suited his temperament anyway. ("I pretty much decided when I graduated high school that I was not cut out for work. I'm workphobic.")

Among the many regulars over the years included Eddie Balchowsky, an American poet, artist and musician who served in the Abraham Lincoln Brigade during the Spanish Civil War. Balchowsky is also among the more than 125 portraits that hang on the ancient walls—all painted by Elliott. Many of the faces are familiar—from Roger Ebert to columnist Mike Royko, John Belushi to Stephen Colbert—while others offer sharp-edged and oftentimes lewd political satire (such as the former Illinois governor Rod Blagojevich being strip searched). The late celebrity chef and travel host Anthony Bourdain liked the late-night dive so much that he featured it on his television show *Anthony Bourdain: Parts Unknown*. Some of the barflies depicted on the wall are not famous, such as Michaela Touhy, who everyone called "Mike" and was commonly referred to as a "character." She was also a regular at O'Rourke's.

Mock posters "depict the bar as if it were the Moulin Rouge….The people in many of his paintings have a sickly yellow green pallor to their faces, suggesting a cartoonish Toulouse-Lautrec," observes Scott Eden. Elliott once told Eden, "The thing about bar life is this: lives tend to be a lot shorter. But on the other hand, there's not a night in this bar I don't have a huge belly laugh. That's the trade-off."[95]

WHAT MAKES A GREAT bartender? Or a great bar?

To veteran *Chicago Tribune* columnist, WGN radio host and author of *A Chicago Tavern: A Goat, a Curse, and the American Dream* Rick Kogan, a good bartender offers "a decent pour, some lively conversation, some decent gossip"; add "a welcoming smile and an understanding ear" for good measure.[96] To Dave Hoekstra, a good bar "is a bouquet of warm memories." Ken Ellis, the Rainbo club bartender, contends, "All you need to do is have liquor in the place, open the doors and treat your customers right. That's all you need to do to get customers coming back."[97]

The EZ Inn at 921 North Western Avenue promotes "Drinks. Hugs. High Fives." Its slogan accentuates the idea that there is no such thing as a stranger at a neighborhood bar. "You are a stranger here but once…" Similarly, Hideout's motto is "Come once and you're a regular."

A HANDFUL OF BARS have become pop culture icons, most famously Billy Goat Tavern, the iconic Lower Michigan Avenue watering hole made famous by *SNL*'s John Belushi. Some come to define a neighborhood.

The Rainbo Club is a shot and beer dive in Ukrainian Village with an interesting history as a polka bar and a favorite of Nelson Algren. Instantly memorable with its wooden bar, tiny stage and red-vinyl booths, over the years the clientele and the neighborhood changed, from prostitutes and junkies to one that was becoming increasingly more bohemian and artsy as the favored haunt of artists, hipsters and musicians. For a short time, it was *the* bar in the neighborhood as a hangout for local rock bands, including Urge Overkill, Tortoise and Eleventh Dream Day. Veruca Salt played, hung out or even worked there. John Haggerty, the guitar player from Naked

Billy Goat Tavern & Grill logo with its stylized man-meets-billy-goat mascot. Actually, the man represented here is the Greek immigrant William "Billy Goat" Sianis, who bought the tavern in 1934 for $205 and whose family still runs the legendary bar. As the sign on the red door to the iconic Lower Michigan Avenue location says, "Butt in Anytime." *Author collection.*

Raygun, worked the bar. But no regular was more famous than Liz Phair (the album cover of her 1993 *Exile in Guyville* was taken in the Rainbo's iconic photo booth). The bar has been around since 1935, and according to legend, it used to be a speakeasy like so many other bars in Chicago. The Rainbo Pub was also where the proposal scene between Rob (John Cusack) and Laura (Danish actress Iben Hjejle) was filmed in Stephen Frears's 2000 film *High Fidelity*. "Drinking lunch on a school day. That's a nice surprise," Laura says with a smirk as the Scottish indie group the Beta Band's song "Dry the Rain" plays softly in the background. (Fun fact: Beta Band keyboardist John Maclean went on to become the director of the critically acclaimed 2015 indie film *Slow West*.)

Musician and Rainbo bartender Tim Kinsella recalled, "People who have probably never seen each other feel like this is their place. This has become shorthand, a meeting place, part of the neighborhood."

Often, going to a bar isn't even about the drinking. It's the camaraderie and the making of connections. Like the traditional coffeehouse, for some it was a place to exchange ideas, to discuss new projects or simply to gossip. The best bars instill a sense of loyalty.

"There's No Other Place in the World Like It"

That's a thought said many times about many places in many places. In this case, it refers to Danny's Tavern. When the online website Block Club reported the closure of the bar, the site received more than seventy-five responses from readers who wanted to—perhaps needed to—share their memories. People had their first dates there. More than a few people described Danny's like "going to someone's apartment." It was like being in someone's house and you were the life of the party, said another.

A big part of the appeal of Danny's was its randomness: according to regulars, you never knew who you were going to meet that night. Regulars included service industry workers, artists, DJs and neighborhood residents. It offered community.

Danny's suffered from a shift in the drinking culture that some critics think coincided with the growth of the Internet. "With the rise of dating apps, weeknight sales began to plummet as singles lost interest in spontaneous real-life meet-ups.…As music streaming apps grew in popularity, the interest in going out to hear live music seemed to wane," wrote Block Club's Hannah Alani.[98]

> ## A Half Dozen Chicago (Area)-Themed Drinking Songs
>
> "Unemployed (Drunk Again)," Michael McDermott from *Last Chance Lounge* (2007)
> "20 Miles South of Nowhere," Michael McDermott from *Bourbon Blue* (2006)
> "Yes, I Guess They Oughta Name a Drink after You," John Prine from *Diamonds in the Rough* (1972)
> "What Made Milwaukee Famous (Made a Loser Out of Me)," Rod Stewart (1972)
> "Hemingway's Whiskey," Guy Clark from *Somedays the Song Writes You* (2009)
> "How Much Tequila (Did I Drink Last Night?)," Steve Goodman from *Affordable Art* (1988)

Danny's Tavern was more than just a candlelit dive bar known for its dance parties and music nights dedicated to the Smiths. It was a literary pub of sorts. It held its popular Danny's Reading Series by poets and authors on the third Wednesday of the month. (Past participants included Mark Strand and Dan Beachy-Quick, author of one of my favorite and quirkiest books, *A Whaler's Dictionary* [Milkweed Editions, 2008], which was inspired by Ishmael's cetological dictionary in *Moby Dick*.) The original owner was indeed a Danny: Daniel Cimaglio. A victim of the pandemic, the bar closed in late 2020.

Lottie, Theresa, Gerri, Wanda, Phyllis and Marie

In 1897, the city council banned female employees who were not related to the owner from working in taverns. The intent was to serve an anti-vice measure, but even so, wives of saloonkeepers continued to serve drinks and even hold liquor licenses despite the ordinance.[99] Given the anti-female sentiment of much of Chicago saloon culture history, it is important to recognize the female bartenders who have contributed to the culture.

Nowadays, it's probably best known as the locale of the fictional firefighters on NBC's *Chicago Fire* television show, where it is known as Molly's,[100] but

Lottie's Pub in Bucktown has been around in some form since as far back as 1928, when it started out as a grocery.

There really was a Lottie: Walter "Lottie" Zagorski. According to the tavern's website, Lottie stood six feet tall and was an intimidating figure not only because of her height but also because of her towering personality. She also happened to be one of the few known transvestites to own a bar in Chicago. A photograph depicts her wearing a flowered muumuu and heels, cigarette in hand. She was known to cuss in a very deep masculine voice.

Zagorski ran strip shows on Saturday nights in the secret basement (access was through a private door). "Algren's money supported much of the gambling bets, and he won big nearly every time."[101] Zagorski's Rathskeller, as it was called, was a favorite of politicians and gangsters alike. Zagorski's operated as a gambling den, house of prostitution and strip tease joint where all-night poker was played. Horse betting, gambling and other vices took place in the basement. Not everyone turned a blind eye though. In 1967, the FBI and IRS raided Zagorski's, finding the hidden rathskeller in the basement. In 1967, Zagorski was arrested on charges of illegal bookkeeping. She died in 1973 of natural causes, but not before she testified before a grand jury. She was never actually charged.

In the 1980s, it was known as Busia's Polish Pub (*busia* is "grandmother" in Polish). In 1986, Bill Lockhart, the new owner, renamed it Lottie's Pub & Grill in honor of Zagorski.

Theresa Needham was the owner of Theresa's Lounge, a tavern that doubled as a blues club located in the basement of 4801 South Indiana Avenue in a yellow-brick apartment building in Bronzeville. She was a bartender, bouncer, booker and owner. Generous to friends and customers, Needham sometimes even lent money to help pay their bills when cash was low or extended credit at the bar.

Despite its not having a proper stage, the best of Chicago blues performed at Theresa's Lounge, including Junior Wells, Muddy Waters, Howlin' Wolf, Big Walter Horton, Memphis Slim, Sunnyland Slim, Elmore James and Buddy Guy. Regulars came every night and treated the tavern like their own living room. It was a home away from home.[102]

Gerri Oliver was another iconic female bar owner. She bought the Palm Tavern at 446 East 47th Street in 1956 and turned it into the center of

Black culture in Chicago. It was a tavern that presented the best in African American talent. Louis Armstrong, Duke Ellington, Lena Horne, Muddy Waters, Count Basie, Quincy Jones, Nat King Cole, Billie Holiday and Dinah Washington all played here. It was also a gathering place where people could talk about politics and current events or just enjoy each other's company. Although it was not a restaurant, Oliver was known to occasionally cook for her patrons, with red beans and rice being the house specialty.

"When I lock these doors for good, that will mark the end of an era," Oliver told Dave Hoekstra. "People of the new era are not like mine. I don't see anyone out here who realizes the historical value of the Palm or has any inkling of history per se."[103]

Oliver has been commemorated in pop culture. In 1998, Fernando Jones wrote *I Was There When the Blues Was Red Hot* about Gerri's; in 2014, Chicago bluesman Billy Branch recorded "Going to See Miss Gerri One More Time" for his *Blues Shock* album.

The Palm Tavern closed in 2001 and was razed in 2004. Oliver died on December 7, 2020, in Palos Verde, California, at the age of 101.

THERE IS NO SIGN outside Stanley's Tavern, a beer and a shot bar, at 4258 South Ashland Avenue in the Back of the Yards neighborhood. It is the last remnant of what was once known as Whiskey Row near the Union Stock Yards. Stanley's Tavern specialized in cheap drafts and hearty lunches.

A Polish immigrant, Stanley Kurek worked at the Stockyards in the pickling division of Wilson & Co. meatpacker. He quit to open his own tavern. His wife, Josephine, also a Polish immigrant, became a barmaid, and their children—well, they helped out too. When daughter Wanda was ten, Stanley bought a building at 43rd and Ashland, tore down the building that was there, built a new one and opened his namesake tavern. He moved the family upstairs. He was all set.

The family offered free lunch (usually sandwiches) during the Depression and then later hot meals, cooked first by Josephine and then by Wanda, such as baked ham with raisin sauce, roast pork with dumplings, stuffed cabbage and potato salad and Cornish hens. "[Wanda] acted as feisty as a Chicago winter but she had the charms of an endless summer."[104] She lived upstairs, and every morning, she opened her father's tavern. Workers from the stockyards would come to the tavern with six-inch pails, fill them up to the brim with beer and then carry them back home. It was an early version of today's growler but heavier and bulkier. Workers could also cash their checks at Stanley's. It was an all-purpose kind of place.

During the days when workers at the stockyards had three shifts, Stanley's Tavern would open as early as 7:00 a.m. and close as late as 2:00 a.m. There was the morning crowd, followed by the lunch crowd and then, finally, the evening trade. "Every building was a bar from 41st Street to 43rd Street," Wanda told Dave Hoekstra. From 1924 until 1983, Stanley's was open seven days a week.

The bar's longevity owes a lot to the personal touch of the Kurek family. Wanda knew everyone in the neighborhood, and they knew her.

Wanda Kurek died in 2019 at the age of ninety-five.

PHYLLIS AND CLEM JASKOT Sr. opened what is now Phyllis' Musical Inn at 1800 West Division Street in Wicker Park in 1954. At the time, it was a polka music club on what was then the Polish Broadway. In 1980, it catered to a country-rock club and finally an old-time bar in a neighborhood that had turned into hipster central.

Phyllis was a coal miner's daughter from Wilkes-Barre, Pennsylvania, who, according to journalist Dave Hoekstra, "came to Chicago on a bus with her suitcase and accordion." Her future husband, Clem, was also from somewhere else—Chippewa Falls, Wisconsin. He was a roofer. They met at what would later become Phyllis' Musical Inn. At the time, she played polkas and waltzes in the various Polish clubs in the neighborhood. "People came from all over," she told Hoekstra. In later years and as musical tastes changed, the Jaskots booked contemporary music and even presented poetry slams.

Like the best of bartenders, Jaskot treated her customers with respect. Hoekstra goes further and says she treated them "as if they were all her children." Perhaps best of all, the Jaskots didn't change the décor. It was as if Phyllis' Musical Inn was stuck in time, which it was.

Phyllis Jaskot died in 2020 at the age of ninety-three.

"SHE MADE YOU FEEL like you belonged," bartender Leo Zak said about Marie Wuczynski, owner of the Bucktown dive bar Marie's Rip Tide Lounge.

Isn't that the best thing anyone could say about a bar owner?

Wuczynski bought the place, located in a nondescript corner off the Kennedy Expressway, in 1961, two years after Hawaii became a state. Initially, she considered giving the bar a Hawaiian theme: leis and drinks with umbrellas and such. But as the daughter of a Polish immigrant, it made more sense "to go Polish" instead. Like other Bucktown/Wicker Park bars with a Polish background, she presented polka bands several times a week. She would also sing herself, tell bawdy jokes and even perform magic tricks. Her goal was to make her customers happy, and by all accounts, she did.

It was everyone's favorite late-night stop for that last nightcap. Bill Murray, John Belushi and Vince Vaughn stopped by when they were in town, but they were not the reason that people came. They were not what made the place special. The regulars were and, of course, Marie herself. What other bar owner has inspired at least two songs? Michael McDermott's "20 Miles South of Nowhere" and Robbie Fulk's "Marie's Rip Tide."

Wuczynski died in 2011 at the age of eighty-eight, in her home above the tavern.

One Last Round

The corner bar offers community, a combination of laughter, noise and joy and what Pete Hamill has called "the leveling democracy of drink."[105] The saloon was an extension of the home. Saloonkeepers knew their neighbors, and neighbors knew one another even if they were not friends in the traditional sense. Maybe they just knew one another from the tavern, but oftentimes that shared sense of recognition—perhaps a nod or a wave as they entered or left the premises—was enough to be considered a part of the community. At its democratic best, the corner bar was among the most egalitarian of public spaces.

Saloonkeepers contributed to the fabric of the neighborhood. When the poor needed a quick infusion of money or a loan, they turned to their local saloonkeeper. After a funeral, mourners would meet at their favorite local.

Where else but the saloon would people come together for public functions? The owner provided services—both alcohol and food—and, if he were a politician himself, exchanged beer and whiskey for votes. Everyone knew the saloonkeeper, and the saloonkeeper knew everyone. Any self-respecting politician knew it was in his best interest to know and befriend his local barkeep. Personal contact was not only the best way to advance up the political ladder, but it was also the best way to get out the vote or, as mentioned earlier, pay for the vote.

The saloon was a social gathering spot and the place not only to hear the local news but also share gossip. The saloonkeeper knew what was going

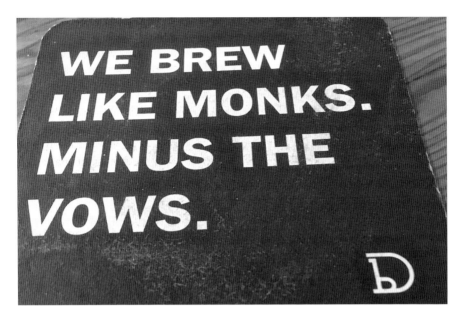

"We Brew Like Monks. Minus the Vows": the cheeky motto of Dovetail Brewery along Ravenswood's Malt Row. Other breweries along the Row and surrounding area include Begyle, Empirical, Half Acre, Smylie Brothers, Spiteful Brewing, Keeping Together, LaGrow Organic Beer Co., Urban Brew Labs and one distillery, Koval. Forbidden Root, Chicago's first botanic brewery, opened in 2021 at the former location of the now shuttered Band of Bohemia brewpub. *Photo by author.*

on in the neighborhood. As we have seen, the saloon was the center of a neighborhood's political life. Political parties and organizations met in saloons or in its upstairs hall. Often, the saloon was the unofficial headquarters of a political party.

Of course, the type of patrons, the ambiance, the overall vibe at a bar can widely vary depending on the time of day. There is a world of difference, for example, between what goes on at noon and what takes place after midnight.

THE LAMENT OF THE vanishing neighborhood tavern has been sung for decades now, and for good reason. Chicago at the height of the saloon culture at the turn of the twentieth century had more than 8,000 saloons. In 2019, the number fell to roughly 870.

So what happened?

After World War II, the neighborhood bar trade was booming again. But times change. Tastes change. People didn't drink the same way they used to, or they worked from home, or when they did work, they would go straight home afterward.

Some of the decline can be attributed to Mayor Richard M. Daley, who was concerned about maintaining or reviving quality of life in the neighborhoods even though when he and his father, Mayor Richard J. Daley, were growing up on the streets of Bridgeport there was virtually a tavern on every corner. Richard J. Daley ran on a law-and-order image, which included ridding the city of public nuisances such as taverns. Worse, taverns could be magnets for crime. Daley, during his more than twenty years in office, revoked the liquor licenses of hundreds upon hundreds of bars.[106] Exercising their local option prerogative, citizens could vote to ban alcohol sales in their precincts. Daley encouraged this. In fact, both father and son were concerned about unruly behavior in taverns. Revocations of liquor licenses and encouraging precincts in the city to vote them dry led to a substantial decline in neighborhood taverns.

Another reason for the decline in the corner bar was demographics. Young people don't drink as much, or they prefer to drink from home. Another is the transient nature of people living in gentrifying neighborhoods. When there is no loyalty to a neighborhood, it is less likely there will be loyalty to a particular tavern.

The decline in the neighborhood tavern parallels and reflects changes in American drinking habits. Refrigeration and air conditioning allowed people to drink at home without going to the corner bar. Overall, people nowadays drink less than their elders did.

When a tavern that has been an indelible part of the neighborhood closes, it is almost like there has been a death in the family. Schaller's Pump in Bridgeport survived for nearly 140 years before shutting down in 2017. A longtime hangout of the Daley clan, it catered to the residents of the neighborhood. "Every happy moment in my family's life has been here," Elmer Mestrovic told the *Tribune*'s Grace Wong and Patrick M. O'Connell. And in the tradition of the old Chicago tavern, Schaller's served food too— plenty of it, including hamburgers, corned beef and liver sausage sandwiches, pork chops, steaks and ribs. "You never left hungry," said Leanne Scanlon.

Brian Friedler decided to close his Bucktown tavern the Artful Dodger in 2005 because he thought it was time. "And, unfortunately," he told the *Tribune*'s Terry Armour, "the neighborhood tavern is dying." Armour seemed to agree. "You know the kind of place," he wrote, "the ones that used to be on just about every corner from Bridgeport to Edgewater, from Sauganash to South Shore." There was nothing special about most of these places.

And that's what made them special: "Just a place to grab a shot and a beer, complain about the Cubs, Sox, and politics."[107]

The Artful Dodger was the kind of corner bar where people met their spouses. Out of loyalty, shared experiences and a genuine fondness, they considered it "their place." Weddings and memorials were held there, even baby showers. Regulars are what make the corner bar a neighborhood bar. In true neighborhood bars, a bond can exist between staff and the regulars. "The bond is real when you have a culture of regulars," says Bill Savage, who used to tend bar at Cunneen's and, earlier, at Hamilton's and has taught courses on Chicago saloon culture at the Newberry Library. "Regulars get to know each other. They're less than best pals but more than acquaintances. There's a sweet spot." Regulars go to the bar as much for the socializing and conversation as for the beer.

Neighborhood bars have a real stake in the community. The owners, the bartenders and the customers care what happens both inside the bar and outside the barroom doors. A good bartender will notice when a regular doesn't show up, for example; oftentimes, they keep track of people when nobody else does. "Bars have an existence beyond the physical space," adds Savage. "Bars can nurture and sustain, and they can distract and destroy. It's all about moderation and balance."

Guthrie's Tavern in Lakeview was another corner bar. After closing down during the COVID-19 pandemic, it rose, like Lazarus, from the dead when economic conditions improved. As *Chicago Tribune* theater critic Chris Jones noted, "You didn't go to Guthrie's to pick someone up. You went to talk with someone you hoped to get to know."[108]

As with all industries, saloon culture of course has its dark side. Bill Savage offers a sobering reminder. "All [the] romanticization of bars (where everybody knows your name) miss the fact that many regulars are just sad drunks, or genuinely not nice people who never quite cross the line of getting banned. In most neighborhood bars, for every regular you're glad to see, there's one you'd never want to see again, if it were possible. [That's] the nature of being open to the public, which includes the full range of humanity." Savage adds, "Bar culture is not well-served by either rose-colored glasses or emphasis on the bad drinkers. Bars are just like any other institution: some are bad, some okay, some good, some great."[109]

Bartenders are accustomed to seeing all kinds of humanity on display—for better or worse. Or, as Dmitry Samarov archly notes in his memoir *Old Style*, bartenders "deal with odd people at off hours."

And yet the corner bar can often represent the best qualities of a neighborhood: loyalty, a sense of real community and belonging as well as the everyday rites of passage associated with a typical human life. Notes *Tribune* columnist Rick Kogan:

> *The relationship between bartenders and their customers can be a special one, a bond born of booze, yes, but also of familiarity and intimacy, for it is with a bartender that many people feel comfortable sharing their hopes and fears, their troubles and triumphs. It is also a vanishing bond, since there are fewer taverns than there used to be and, though you can still find some men and women who have been serving drinks for decades, tending bar is no longer seen as a lifelong livelihood for young people, many of whom feel compelled to gild the definition of their task by calling themselves mixologists.*[110]

One More for the Road

And yet, like a small miracle, the corner bar lives on, despite everything, because it serves as a sanctuary for neighbors, friends, family and temporary strangers to come together. It persists because of good company and the promise that it presents but also because of the importance of place.

The corner bar functions as the economic engine of a city block. It adds to the social and emotional adhesion of the wider neighborhood. As we have seen, the best of them can be an extension of home, which is why so many regulars describe their favorite bar like being in their own living room. They cut across age, class, race and sexual orientation barriers. Corner bars are democratic oases of talk and laughter and, occasionally, argument. It's the place where you can tell secrets—or lies—knowing or, more likely, hoping that whatever words pass through your lips will never leave the confines of the space. J.R. Moehringer, in his memoir, *The Tender Bar*, equates bars with love affairs. They depend "on a delicate mix of timing, chemistry, lighting, luck and—maybe above all—generosity."[111]

The quintessential corner bar embodies not only the essence of a neighborhood, of a block, but it is also the place where the entire life cycle—its customs, traditions and rituals—can play out, from the celebration of births, marriages and achievements to the commemoration of the loss of loved ones. That's when the corner bar becomes more than just a neighborhood anchor or a local institution but something else much more profound—something sacred and precious and worthy in its own right.

And that's enough.

RESOURCES

Brewseum
www.chicagobrewseum.org

The Chicago Brewseum highlights the dynamic culture and innovative history of one of the world's most vibrant industries. By using stories of the past and tales of the present, the Chicago Brewseum takes a deeper look into one of the oldest beverages and its power to build community and its importance as an ongoing cultural force. The board of directors consists of a who's who in Chicago craft beer. In addition to Liz Garibay, other members include Andres Araya of 5 Rabbit, John Hall of Goose Island, Tracy Hurst of Metropolitan, Gabriel Magliaro of Half Acre, Dan Oliver of the Chicago History Museum and Michael Roper of Hopleaf. The National Advisory Board includes author-historian Karen Abbott, cicerone and contributor to *The Oxford Companion to Beer* Ray Daniels, Josh Deth of Revolution Brewing, Karen Hamilton of Lagunitas, Russell Lewis of the Chicago History Museum, author Randy Mosher and Northwestern University professor Bill Savage.

Chicago Beer Experience
www.chicagobeerexperience.com

Offers Chicago beer–tasting and bar tours with a touch of history. Also offers beer-tasting classes and private tours for six or more people any day of the week.

Resources

Chicago Beer Society
www.chibeer.org

Founded in 1977 as a nonprofit educational association dedicated to the appreciation of beer.

History on Tap
www.historyontap.com

Liz Garibay created History on Tap in 2002, a project that explores history through the lens of alcohol. As the public historian at the Chicago History Museum, she created an array of unique programming, including History Pub Crawls, an innovative approach to learning and one that combined education with socialization.

Pocket Guide to Hell

Produced from 2008 to 2015 by Paul Durica, a former graduate student at the University of Chicago and now director of exhibitions at the Newberry Library, Pocket Guide to Hell was a series of free and interactive public talks, walking tours and historical reenactments that focused on Chicago's past. Past reenactments with a drinking theme include the Whitechapel Club in 2011, the First Ward Ball in 2013 and the 160th anniversary of the Lager Beer Riot in 2015. Pocket Guide to Hell continues to provide walking tours and collaborations with individuals and institutions on public history projects. For more information, email pocketguidetohell@gmail.com.

A Subjective List of Classic Chicago Bars

Billy Goat Tavern
(Lower 430 North Michigan Avenue)

A destination bar and probably the most famous bar in Chicago—thanks to John "Cheezborger! Cheezborger! Cheezborger!" Belushi. To read all about it—including the Billy Goat Curse—see Rick Kogan's *A Chicago Tavern: A Goat, a Curse, and the American Dream*. In 2020, Billy Goat partnered with the Darien, Illinois–based Miskatonic Brewing to create Billy Goat IPA and Billy Goat Pilsner.

Burwood Tap
(724 West Wrightwood Avenue)

Established in 1933 and located on a leafy residential street, it is said to be the second-oldest bar in Chicago. The Burwood is a true corner bar—literally. According to Sean Parnell's Chicago Bar Project website, one of its regulars was Leroy Brown, the hero of the 1973 Jim Croce song, "Bad, Bad Leroy Brown."

A Subjective List of Classic Chicago Bars

Chief O'Neill's Pub & Restaurant
(3471 North Elston Avenue)

An Irish pub and live Irish music venue and the only pub in Chicago—or perhaps anywhere—named after a police officer. An Irish immigrant from County Cork, Chief Francis O'Neill was the chief of police, but more importantly, he was also a musician and a collector of traditional Irish tunes. It has a large beer garden.

Clark Street Ale House
(742 North Clark Street)

A friendly and unpretentious River North tavern. Everyone is welcome—whether human or animal. The back wall features a hand-painted mural depicting the history of brewing in Chicago.

Cunneen's
(1425 West Devon Avenue)

If you had any doubt that this is a traditional corner bar, the Old Style sign hanging outside dispels all notions. This East Rogers Park watering hole is known for its cheap beer, eclectic décor (that would include a wooden Indian) and laid-back atmosphere. It's also famous for its "celebrity" bartenders, which included folk singer Ed Holstein, whose brother ran the folk club Holsteins on Lincoln Avenue, and author and university professor Bill Savage, who tended bar there for nearly thirty years before retiring in 2015. Don't forget to check out the fiery-red Richard J. Daley clock that hovers above the bar.

Duke of Perth
(2913 North Clark Street)

The one and only Scottish pub in the city. It is owned by Scots natives (and cousins) Jack Crombie and Colin Cameron and is the only place in town for those in dire need of a haggis burger. It is a proud recipient of the honor of being named a "Great Whisky Bar of the World."

A Subjective List of Classic Chicago Bars

Green Door Tavern
(678 North Orleans Street)

The building is old—it was built just after the Chicago Fire—and it was the last wood-frame building allowed in the central district center. Its age is apparent too in its creaky structure—the building does lean a bit, which only adds to its worn charm. The tavern itself opened in 1921. Chock-full of Americana, it is a sight to behold. In the basement in the adjacent building is another wonder—the Drifter, a speakeasy-cum-classic-cocktail bar.

Guthrie's Tavern
(1300 West Addison Street)

A beloved Wrigleyville bar that rose from the dead. After closing in 2020 during the pandemic, it miraculously reopened in 2021. During Prohibition, it was a grocery store, but it has been a tavern in one way or another since 1933. One of its best features is its sign, which depicts a cheerful, gaily dressed gentleman in a red vest and green jacket sitting beside a small table, his hand clutching a beer.

Hopleaf Bar
(5148 North Clark Street)

A mecca for craft beer fans in Andersonville and beyond inspired by the beer and food culture of Belgium. Owner Mike Roper epitomizes the best of bar culture by creating a great bar that caters to the needs of the neighborhood. "We're true publicans," he told the *Tribune*'s Josh Noel, "operating the way taverns existed in the 17th century."

Kasey's Tavern
(701 South Dearborn Street)

A Printers Row local that boasts the second-oldest liquor license in the city: a bar has occupied this location for more than one hundred years.

A Subjective List of Classic Chicago Bars

Longman & Eagle
(2657 North Kedzie Avenue)

Its motto says it all: "Eat. Sleep. Whiskey." But it also has bourbon, house cocktails and, of course, beer. The fresh and seasonal bar food is above par: in 2010, Michelin gave it a star (former chef Jared Wentworth has since moved on to the Michelin-starred Moody Tongue in the South Loop). In the spirit of Mark Beaubien's Sauganash Hotel, it offers six rooms on the second floor.

Map Room
(1949 North Hoyne Avenue)

An unpretentious corner bar with distinction: it bills itself as a "traveler's tavern" (its motto is "Drink local, think global"). Like Avondale's Sleeping Village, it is serves coffee in the morning. The latter tavern, though, also presents live music at night.

Marge's Still
(1758 North Sedgwick Avenue)

Established in 1885, Marge's is considered the oldest continually running tavern in Chicago. In 1957, Marge Landeck became the first woman in the city to obtain a liquor license. She was the owner as well as the bartender and bouncer, when necessary. She also reportedly brewed bathtub gin on the second floor. The current owners serve Prohibition era–themed cocktails. In its earlier reincarnation, it was simply Marge's Pub.

Maria's Packaged Goods & Community Bar
(960 West 31st Street)

Start with a "slashie" (half bar/half liquor store) and add one of the best selections of craft beer and a community canteen, and you get the essence of community or, as the owners call it, "radical hospitality." And don't forget the Marz taproom at 3630 South Iron Street.

A Subjective List of Classic Chicago Bars

Queen Mary Tavern
(2125 West Division Street)

It was not named after Mary, Queen of Scots, or any other monarch but rather for a different queen, building owner Mary Kafka, who operated the bar with her husband until 1975. After being shuttered for a time, this neighborhood cocktail tavern that dates back to the 1950s reopened under new owners Matt Eisler and Kevin Heisner with Mary's blessing and a British maritime theme. Its motto? Stand Fast the Holy Ghost.

Red Lion Pub
(2446 North Lincoln Avenue)

The revamped and modernized Red Lion retains the historic atmosphere of the original pub. Proprietor and bartender extraordinaire Colin Cordwell has added his personal collection of books, including a wall dedicated to his late father, John Cordwell, a highly acclaimed architect who opened the original Red Lion in 1984. In 1986, Chicago Shakespeare Theatre made its debut with its first production of *Henry IV* on the roof of the original Red Lion (it has since moved to a bigger pad, at Navy Pier). The upstairs space also presented readings and open-mic comedies. Alas, the current pub does not boast the same kind of space for such public activities, although it does have a private balcony room that fits ten to twenty people. It is said to be haunted.

Twin Anchors
(1655 North Sedgwick Street)

Founded in 1932, Twin Anchors is an iconic pub and rib joint in a building that dates back to at least 1881 and is now run by the Tuzi family. A former speakeasy, it was established by two members of the Chicago Yacht Club—hence the nautical name and theme. It was said to be favorite hangout of Ol' Blues Eyes himself, Frank Sinatra, during the 1960s and 1970s when he was in town.

A Subjective List of Classic Chicago Bars

And many more, including Bangers & Lace, Billy Sunday, California Clipper, Carol's Pub, Cork & Kerry, Delilah's, Four Moon Tavern, Globe Pub, Gingerman Tavern (well, okay, GMan Tavern, if you insist), Grafton Pub & Grill, Haymarket Pub, the House of Glunz, Ina Mae Tavern & Packaged Goods, Long Room, Matchbox, Miller's Pub, Monk's Pub, Moody's Pub, Owen & Engine, Pleasant House Pub, Scofflaw, Sheffield's, Simone's, Skylark, Ten Cat and Will's Northwoods Inn.

A Triptych of the Best Fictional Bars with Chicago Connections

- The bar in *Call Northside 777* starring James Stewart. Saloon scholar Bill Savage has called this 1948 film noir classic "the most realistic depiction of historic Chicago bars."
- The Weir in Steppenwolf Theater's 2000–01 production of Conor McPherson's play of the same name. The pub was a replica of an Irish country pub in County Laois. According to *Tribune* writer Anne Taubeneck, the Steppenwolf version consisted of liquor shelves full of diluted, unsweetened iced tea masquerading as whiskey; diluted root beer as brandy; and watered-down grape juice as white wine. On the other hand, the till and cash were filled with real Irish money. As far as the beer is concerned, the Harp's tap dispensed nonalcoholic Sharp's.
- Roddy Doyle's nameless Irish pub in *Two Pints*. In March 2019, Chicago Shakespeare Theater presented Doyle's two-man play about two friends drinking and philosophizing on life and loss in its own warm and cozy pub located off the lobby.

NOTES

Chapter 1

1. For many years, John Kinzie was even called the Father of Chicago, but Jean Baptiste Point du Sable now holds that distinction.
2. Perry Duis, *The Saloon: Public Drinking in Chicago and Boston, 1880–1920* (Urbana: University of Illinois Press, 1998), 10.
3. John Dean Caton, *Miscellanies* (Boston: Houghton, Osgood and Company, 1880), 86.
4. Caldwell, or Sauganash, is prominent for another reason. It was Caldwell who secured the peace between the Native American population and the early white settlers in the Treaty of 1835.
5. Beer historian Bob Skilnik spells the name "Diversy," but the street name that honors him retains the second "e." For a time there was a tavern named after him, the short-lived Michael Diversey's at 670 West Diversey Parkway in Lincoln Park.
6. Skilnik, "Building Chicago Was Thirsty Work," *Chicago Tribune*, July 16, 1997.
7. Country music producer and songwriter Glenn Sutton turned the phrase into the song "What's Made Milwaukee Famous (Has Made a Loser Out of Me)." In 1968, Jerry Lee Lewis had a top-10 hit with it on *Billboard*'s country charts, while Rod Stewart's version reached no. 4 in 1972 on the UK charts.

8. Dr. Brian Alberts and Liz Garibay, Newberry Library seminar, "From Bier to Beer: How Germans Made Lagers 'King' in the Midwest," July 20, 2019.
9. One could argue that at least one tied house remains in the Chicago area: Wild Onion Tied House in nearby Oak Park, Illinois, operated by the Kainz family, who have a strong history of beer brewing dating back to Prohibition. The Wild Onion Tied House is "tied" to the family's Wild Onion Brewery located in Lake Barrington, Illinois.
10. Daniel Okrent, *Last Call: The Rise and Fall of Prohibition* (New York: Scribner), 29.
11. Commission on Chicago Landmarks, "Five Schlitz Brewery Tied-Houses," April 7, 2011, 14.
12. In 1908, the Illinois Supreme Court ordered the company to sell its property. The South Pullman District, between 111th and 115th Streets and Cottage Grove and Langley Avenues, was designated a national landmark in 1971 and a Chicago landmark on October 16, 1972.
13. Argus specialized in lagers and pilsners. One of its pilsners was the Paschke Pils, brewed in honor of the Chicago artist Ed Paschke (1939–2004). The beer's label art came from his collection.
14. Commission on Chicago Landmarks, "Five Schlitz Brewery Tied-Houses," 18.

Chapter 2

15. Perry Duis, "The Saloon in a Changing Chicago," *Chicago History*, Winter 1975–76, 220.
16. Duis, *Saloon*, 131.
17. For a thorough history of Mike McDonald and his time, see Lindberg, *Gambler King of Clark Street*.
18. O'Leary owned the four-story mansion at 726 West Garfield Avenue. It was built in 1885 for his mother—the famous, or infamous, Catherine O'Leary, whose cow that kicked over a lantern was said to have started the 1871 Great Chicago Fire. (It was later learned that it was all a ruse; a local reporter confessed years later to making it up. By then, of course, the damage was done.) In early 2021, the historic nineteenth-century O'Leary mansion in the Englewood neighborhood was for sale. At 6,720 square feet, the eighteen-bed, ten-bath dwelling was listed for $535,700. It was the only property in Chicago to have its own dedicated fire hydrant.

Another unique feature: the secret tunnel that once connected the mansion to another house next door. For background on John "Mushmouth" Johnson, see also Michael La Pointe, "The Black Gambling King of Chicago," *Paris Review*, April 17, 2020.

19. Lloyd Wendt and Herman Kogan, *Lords of the Levee: The Story of Bathhouse John and Hinky Dink* (Evanston, IL: Northwestern University Press, 2005), 74.
20. Ibid., 73.
21. Ken Suskin Report, December 25, 2007, www.kennethsuskin.blogspot.com.
22. Wendt and Kogan, *Lords of the Levee*, 336 and 337.
23. Ibid., 283.
24. Karen Abbott, *Sin in the Second City: Madams, Playboys, and the Battle for America's Soul* (New York: Random House, 2008), 58.
25. "Ten Indicted in Diabolisms of 'Mickey Finn,'" *Tribune*, July 9, 1918; William Lee, "Police: Milwaukee Women Drugged, Robbed Men," *Chicago Tribune*, October 21, 2020.
26. Abbott, *Sin in the Second City*, 12.
27. William T. Stead was on board the *Titanic* when it sank on April 15, 1912. His body was never found.
28. Wendt and Kogan, *Lords of the Levee*, 156. Despite the slight difference in spelling, could Hinky Dink's colorful word "lallapalooza" be the inspiration behind the annual four-day music festival held each summer in Grant Park that attracts thousands? According to Merriam-Webster, the official definition of the word is "one that is extraordinarily impressive"/"an outstanding example." Its origin is unknown, although it does date back to 1896, the heyday of Hinky Dink and Bathhouse John. Hmmm.
29. Wendt and Kogan, *Lords of the Levee*, 268–69.
30. Abbott, *Sin in the Second City*, 234.
31. Duis, "Saloon in a Changing Chicago," 224.
32. Abbott, *Sin in the Second City*, 230.
33. The former Everleigh Club at 2447 North Halsted was a popular Lincoln Park tavern—and a mainstay of the Lincoln Park pub crawl—named after the famous sisters. It closed in the late 1990s.
34. Wendt and Kogan, *Lords of the Levee*, 356.
35. June Sawyers, "Atlas Obscura's First Ward Ball Celebrates Chicago's Bawdy Levee District History," *Third Coast Review*, January 29, 2019.

Chapter 3

36. Okrent, *Last Call*, 373.
37. Skilnik, "Building Chicago Was Thirsty Work."
38. Okrent, *Last Call*, 26.
39. Susan Cheever, *Drinking in America: Our Secret History* (New York: Twelve/Grand Central Publishing, 2015), 146.
40. George Ade, *The Old-Time Saloon: Not Wet—Not Dry, Just History*, edited and introduced by Bill Savage (Chicago: University of Chicago Press, 2016), 100.
41. Bill Savage quoted in Ade, *Old-Time Saloon*, 186.
42. Okrent, *Last Call*, 16.
43. Cheever, *Drinking in America*, 140.
44. Okrent, *Last Call*, 18–19. Temperance Beer Company in Evanston, just over the Chicago border, cheekily takes its name from the temperance movement. Evanston was a dry community from 1858 until 1972. What's more, suffragist and temperance reformer and president of the Woman's Christian Temperance Union (WCTU) Frances Willard lived in Evanston. The Frances Willard House, also referred to as the Rest Cottage, opened as a museum in 1900.
45. Okrent, *Last Call*, 97.
46. Christopher M. Elias, *Gossip Men: J. Edgar Hoover, Joe McCarthy, Roy Cohn, and the Politics of Insinuation* (Chicago: University of Chicago Press, 2021), 35.
47. Okrent, *Last Call*, 37.
48. Rachel E. Bohlmann, "Local Option," in *The Encyclopedia of Chicago*, edited by James Grossman, Ann Durkin Keating and Janice L. Reiff (Chicago: University of Chicago Press, 2004), 490–91.
49. Bob Skilnik, *The History of Brewing in Chicago: 1833–1978* (Fort Lee, NJ: Barricade Books, 2006), 90.
50. Ibid., 104.
51. Ibid., 128.
52. The Chicago Historical Society, as it was then called, did not acquire Kenna's famous schooner until 1954. According to John Clayton, Kenna initially kept one for himself. Then, in 1924, he gave it to Anna Gordon, president of the WCTU. Apparently, she was not offended by the gift but rather found some humor in the irony of receiving it and even held a luncheon at the organization's headquarters in Evanston, Illinois, which is now the Frances Willard Home and Museum. See John Clayton, "The

Scourge of Sinners: Arthur Burrage Farwell," *Chicago History* 3, no. 2 (Fall 1974): 74 and 76–77.
53. Abbott, *Sin in the Second City*, 55.
54. Skilnik, *History of Brewing in Chicago*, 127.
55. Ibid., 137.
56. The punk–new wave bar O'Banion's in River North took its name from the gangster Dion O'Banion. Located at 661 North Clark Street, it was originally a gay bar. It began presenting live music in 1979 even though it had no stage (later, a small platform was added). The short-lived club hosted some of the biggest names in punk, including Hüsker Dü, the Dead Kennedys and the Replacements, as well as local punk bands Naked Raygun and Skafish and later the new-wave band Bohemia. It is now the vastly different Kerryman, a lovely Irish bar. In a previous life, it was called McGovern's Saloon, a hangout for the likes of Bugs Moran, a former ally of O'Banion.
57. Skilnik, *History of Brewing in Chicago*, 133.
58. Ibid., 149.
59. Ibid., 150.
60. Okrent, *Last Call*, 26.
61. The St. Valentine's Day Massacre victims were two brothers, Peter Gusenberg and Frank Gusenberg, as well as Albert Kachellek, Adam Heyer, Reinhardt Schwimmer, Albert Weinshank and John May.
62. Okrent, *Last Call*, 207.
63. Ibid., 209.
64. Ibid., 211.
65. In 1970, the National Organization for Women (NOW) lawyers Faith Seidenberg and Karen DeCrow filed a discrimination case against McSorley's Old Ale House in New York after they were refused service the year before. The ruling led to a city ordinance banning discrimination against women in public places. The first female patron at McSorley's was Barbara Shaum.
66. It seems like every bar in Chicago tries to play up its speakeasy past, even when the history is dubious. Being a former speakeasy still has cachet. "I never trust rumors about historical locations," Richard Lindberg told me. Email to author, May 17, 2021. Paul Durica arrives at a similar conclusion. "I don't know the number of speakeasies and imagine it's impossible to determine." E-mail to author, September 16, 2021.
67. According to Richard Lindberg, the Merry Gangsters Literary Society met monthly in the 1990s at various places around town but mostly at

Tommy Gun's Garage to talk about Chicago's sordid past. Members included Rich Lindberg, Bill Helmer, Bill Reilly and Nathan Kaplan. Kaplan also edited their newsletter, the *Prohibition Era Times*. They started out small, and eventually "we had a room full of kooks, crime buffs, reporters, cops and even a few criminals," said Lindberg. Guests included the "genial" thief Joseph "Pops" Panczko (according to his obituary, he was arrested more than two hundred times between 1940 and 1994), adult bookstore and massage parlor owner "Weird" Harold Rubin, Richard J. Daley's press secretary Frank Sullivan, WCFL deejay Ron Britain and *Chicago Tribune* crime reporters John O'Brien and Edward Baumann. Email to author, May 16, 2021.
68. Dee-Ann Durbin, "Sober Bars Serving Up Buzz," *Chicago Tribune*, March 19, 2021.
69. Josh Noel, "Don't Sneer at This Beer Anymore," *Chicago Tribune*, January 24, 2021.
70. Grace Wong, "Just Opened: What to Eat and Drink at the Hoxton," *Chicago Tribune*, April 11, 2019.

Chapter 4

71. Skilnik, *History of Brewing in Chicago*, 223.
72. Ibid., 225.
73. Ibid., 211.
74. Ibid., 213.
75. Ibid., 212.
76. Josh Noel, *Barrel-Aged Stout and Selling Out: Goose Island, Anheuser-Busch, and How Craft Beer Became Big Business* (Chicago: Chicago Review Press, 2018), 31.
77. For a complete history of Goose Island, see Josh Noel's excellent *Barrel-Aged Stout and Selling Out*.
78. As of this writing, the Brewers Association listed 283 craft breweries in Illinois and 66 craft breweries in Chicago. In 2020, California had the most craft breweries in the United States.
79. Communication with author.
80. Reinheitsgebot, or the Beer Purity Law, was a decree issued by Duke Wilhelm IV of Bavaria in 1516 that declared that beer would contain only barley, hops and water.
81. Ben Ustick told me: "Turning such a big ship takes time, but Lisa [Zimmer at Miller] was relentless and John [Laffler] was stubborn and

cases of High Life kept showing up at the brewery. Then in June of 2016, John went up to Miller in Milwaukee to learn the secrets of the Lady in the Moon, brewed a ludicrously small ten-barrel batch of High Life on their pilot system and drank a bunch of High Life. Needless to say, he was giddy. Shortly thereafter, Miller's R&D brewers came down, and we brewed Eeek! here in Chicago…and drank a bunch of High Life before drinking even more High Life at Sportsman's Club. Our first batch was released in October 2016. Eeek! has been so successful not only because it was unexpected and challenged the big beer/small beer narrative but, most importantly, because it is a really good beer. The idea of taking these quality High Life ingredients and showcasing them in a different way was an opportunity we did not treat lightly. We wanted this beer to be more than a curiosity, to really stand on its own merits. We believe it does."

Chapter 5

82. See Ray Oldenburg, *The Great Good Place* (New York: Paragon House, 1989).
83. Duis, "Saloon in a Changing Chicago."
84. Chapin & Gore Building is a historic building located at 63 East Adams Street. The distilling company of Chapin & Gore had the building constructed in 1904. The original building consisted of a first-floor bar and store and offices with warehouse space used in the rest of the building. It later combined its warehouse and office space with a street-level retail store and bar. The building was listed in the National Register of Historic Places in 1979 and later designated a Chicago landmark in January 1982. It is now the home of the Symphony Center.
85. John Drury, *Dining in Chicago* (New York: John Day Company, 1931), 34.
86. Duis, *Saloon*, 129.
87. Dominic Pacyga, *American Warsaw: The Rise, Fall, and Rebirth of Polish Chicago* (Chicago: University of Chicago Press, 2019), 261.
88. The Wabansia building was razed when the Kennedy Expressway was built.
89. In 1989, a handful of Algren enthusiasts, including Stuart McCarrell and Warren Leming, formed the Nelson Algren Committee to honor and celebrate his work. The first meeting took place in the basement of Lottie's Pub, where Leming's Chicago Cabaret Ensemble performed Algren's short story "How the Devil Came Down Division Street." Two years later, at the 1991 celebration, Mark Blottner's fifteen-minute film adaptation of "Devil" was shown at the Bop Shop (1807 West Division Street). In 2015,

Blottner and Ilko Davidov co-directed the documentary *Nelson Algren: The End Is Nothing, the Road Is All*. See June Sawyers, "Celebrating the Man with the Golden Pen," *Chicago Tribune*, November 15, 1991; Jeff Huebner, "Full Nelson," *Chicago Reader*, November 19, 1998. The contemporary writer who best exhibits the spirit of Algren is Stuart Dybek. See his wonderful short story collection *The Coast of Chicago*, originally published in 1990.

90. "Last Saturday evening there was a great argument in the Polonia Bar. All the biggest drunks on Division were there, trying to decide who the biggest drunk of them was." Nelson Algren, from "The Devil Came Down Division Street."

91. During the 1960s and 1970s, the Old Corral dive bar in Topanga Canyon, one of Los Angeles's canyon communities, hosted local musicians Canned Heat and Taj Mahal. Its regulars included the likes of Linda Ronstadt, Jimi Hendrix, Janis Joplin and Joni Mitchell. Jamie Lowe, "In Fire-Prone Canyon, Threat of Catastrophe Is the Norm," *New York Times*, June 20, 2021.

92. Josh Noel, "Is the Pandemic Issuing Last Call?" *Chicago Tribune*, August 9, 2020.

93. Mike Seely, "Dive Bars Aren't Down for the Count," *New York Times*, November 12, 2020.

94. Hannah Edgar, "Remarkable Life of Art Castillo and Moulin Jimmy's," *Chicago Reader*, December 10, 2020.

95. Scott Eden, "Drink Here Long Enough and They'll Give You the Bar," *Chicago Reader*, November 9, 2006.

96. Quoted in Chris Jones, "Ed Judge, Dentist Who Chose to Tend Bar at Petterino's," *Chicago Tribune*, March 8, 2021.

97. Patrick Sisson, "Getting to Know Rainbo Club through Its Regulars," *Eater Chicago*, October 1, 2012.

98. Hannah Alani, "Danny's Tavern, Beloved Bucktown Bar since 1986, Closing Permanently," Block Club, November 5, 2020.

99. Duis, *Saloon*, 49.

100. A replica Molly's was built on the Cinespace soundstage in Douglas Park, although the bar is still used for exterior shots.

101. Kali Joy Cramer, *Sinister Chicago: Windy City Secrets, Urban Legends, and Sordid Characters* (Guilford, CT: Globe Pequot, 2020), 154.

102. In 2010, the Black Ensemble Theater presented *Nothing but the Blues*, a tribute to Needham and Theresa's Lounge that featured a five-piece band performing two dozen blues songs. In 2015, the John Primer Band celebrated Needham's birthday at Rosa's Lounge. In 2021, blues singer and guitarist Joanna Connor released an album that honored Needham

with *4801 South Indiana Avenue*. Blues vocalist and harmonica player Junior Wells's live show at Theresa's took place in January 1975 but was not released as a recording until 2006 on the Delmark label.
103. Dave Hoekstra, "Gerri Oliver's Palm Tavern," December 9, 2020. www.davehoestra.com.
104. Dave Hoekstra, "Beauty of Wanda's Stock Yards Bar," June 19, 2019. www.davehoekstra.com.
105. See Pete Hamill, *A Drinking Life: A Memoir* (New York: Back Bay Books, 1994).
106. Jake Smith, "Tavern on (Almost) Every Corner," April 6, 2019, www.wbez.org. Patrick Reardon claims that during the first fifteen years of Richard M. Daley's reign, he removed the licenses of some 1,000 liquor establishments. When Daley was elected mayor in 1989, the city had 3,300 bars. See Patrick Reardon, "Tapped Out," *Chicago Tribune Sunday Magazine*, June 13, 2004.
107. Terry Armour, "Neighborly Artful Dodger Says Goodbye," *Chicago Tribune*, July 14, 2005.
108. Chris Jones, "Goodbye to Guthrie's Tavern," *Chicago Tribune*, July 22, 2020.
109. Bill Savage, email to the author, May 31, 2021. In an earlier conversation about the differences between a welcoming corner bar and an insular, territorial one, he told me, "When everyone turns when you walk in, that's tribal culture." May 8, 2017.
110. Rick Kogan, "At News of the Death of a Bartender, Memories of O'Rourke's," *Chicago Tribune*, October 11, 2018.
111. J.R. Moehringer, *The Tender Bar: A Memoir* (New York: Hachette Books, 2015), 8.

BIBLIOGRAPHY

Abbott, Karen. *Sin in the Second City: Madams, Ministers, Playboys, and the Battle for America's Soul*. New York: Random House, 2008.

Acitelli, Tom. *The Audacity of Hops: The History of America's Craft Beer Revolution*. Chicago: Chicago Review Press, 2013.

Ade, George. *The Old-Time Saloon: Not Wet—Not Dry, Just History*. Edited and Introduced by Bill Savage. Chicago: University of Chicago Press, 2016.

Alani, Hannah. "'There's No Other Place in the World Like Danny's': Chicago Mourns the Loss of a Legendary Bucktown Bar." Block Club, November 13, 2020.

Algren, Nelson. *Chicago City on the Make*. 60th Anniversary Edition. With an introduction by Studs Terkel. Annotated by David Schmittgens and Bill Savage. Chicago: University of Chicago Press, 2001.

Anderson, Mark W. "Tapped Out." Gapers Block: Detour/Chicago, July 16, 2003.

Asbury, Herbert. *Gem of the Prairie: An Informal History of the Chicago Underworld*. New York: Alfred A. Knopf, 1940.

Bohlmann, Rachel E. "Local Option." In *The Encyclopedia of Chicago*. Edited by James R. Grossman, Ann Durkin Keating and Janice L. Reiff. Chicago: University of Chicago Press, 2004.

Carson, Ciaran. *Last Night's Fun: In and Out of Time with Irish Music*. New York: North Point Press/Farrar, Straus and Giroux, 1998.

Bibliography

Caton, John Dean. *Miscellanies*. Boston: Houghton, Osgood and Company, 1880.

Cheever, Susan. *Drinking in America: Our Secret History*. New York: Twelve/Grand Central Publishing, 2015.

Clark, Jack. "Dead Poet's Society: Old Bars Don't Die, They Just Move Away." *Chicago Reader*, February 24, 2000.

Commission on Chicago Landmarks. "Five Schlitz Brewery Tied-Houses and One Schlitz Brewery Stable Building." April 7, 2011.

Cramer, Kali Joy. *Sinister Chicago: Windy City Secrets, Urban Legends, and Sordid Characters*. Guilford, CT: Globe Pequot, 2020.

De La Croix, St. Sukie. *Chicago Whispers: A History of LGBT Chicago before Stonewall*. Madison: University of Wisconsin Press, 2012.

Drury, John. *Dining in Chicago*. Foreword by Carl Sandburg. New York: John Day Company, 1931.

Duis, Perry. "The Saloon in a Changing Chicago." *Chicago History*, Winter 1975–76.

———. *The Saloon: Public Drinking in Chicago and Boston, 1880–1920*. Urbana: University of Illinois Press, 1998.

Durbin, Dee-Ann. "Sober Bars Serving Up Buzz." *Chicago Tribune*, March 19, 2021.

Durica, Paul, and Bill Savage, eds. *Chicago by Day and Night: The Pleasure Seeker's Guide to the Paris of America*. Evanston, IL: Northwestern University Press, 2013.

Edgar, Hannah. "The Remarkable Life of Art Castillo and Moulin Jimmy's." *Chicago Reader*, December 10, 2020.

Elias, Christopher M. *Gossip Men: J. Edgar Hoover, Joe McCarthy, Roy Cohn, and the Politics of Insinuation*. Chicago: University of Chicago Press, 2021.

Fecile, John. "How Chicago Bars Got So Many Old Style Signs." NPR/WBEZ, December 30, 2019.

Fremon, David K. *Chicago Politics Ward by Ward*. Bloomington: Indiana University Press, 1988.

Galil, Leor. "Chicago Punk Was Born Queer." *Chicago Reader*, June 23, 2020.

Golden, Jamie Nesbitt. "Mrs. O'Leary's 1880s Englewood Mansion for Sale—And It Has Its Very Own Fire Hydrant." Block Club, February 16, 2021.

Griffin, Richard T. "Big Jim O'Leary: 'Gambler Boss in the Yards.'" *Chicago History*, Winter 1976–77.

Bibliography

Grossman, James R., Ann Durkin Keating and Janice L. Reiff, eds. *The Encyclopedia of Chicago*. Chicago: University of Chicago Press, 2004.

Haddix, Carol Mighton, Bruce Kraig and Colleen Taylor Sen, eds. *The Chicago Food Encyclopedia*. Foreword by Russell Lewis. Urbana: University of Illinois Press, 2017.

Hamill, Pete. *A Drinking Life: A Memoir*. New York: Back Bay Books, 1994.

Hansen, Harry. *Midwest Portraits: A Book of Memories and Friendships*. New York: Harcourt, Brace, 1923.

Hayner, Don, and Tom McNamee. *Streetwise Chicago: A History of Chicago Street Names*. Foreword by John Callaway. Chicago: Loyola University Press, 1988.

Hennessy, Maggie. "Chicago History Lives in Its Dive Bars." *Fifty Grande*, October 1, 2020.

Hoekstra, Dave. "The Beauty of Wanda's Stock Yards Bar." June 19, 2019. www.davehoekstra.com.

———. "Phyllis Jaskot, Queen of Division Street 1926–2020." November 22, 2020. www.davehoekstra.com.

———. "Gerri Oliver's Palm Tavern Rip." December 9, 2020. www.davehoekstra.com.

Iseman, Courtney. "How a Beer Historian Is Documenting COVID-19's Impact on Brewing: The Biggest Blow to Beer since Prohibition." *Gastro Obscura*, June 5, 2020.

Johnson, Curt, with R. Craig Sautter. *Wicked City—Chicago: From Kenna to Capone*. Highland Park, IL: December Press, 1994.

Jones, Chris. "Chicago Invented Improv. Did Mother's Invent the Singles Bar?" *Chicago Tribune*, November 27, 2013.

———. "Ed Judge, Dentist Who Chose to Tend Bar at Petterino's, Dead at 75." *Chicago Tribune*, March 8, 2021.

———. "Goodbye to Guthrie's Tavern, the First-Date Capital of Wrigleyville." *Chicago Tribune*, July 22, 2020.

Kehoe, Tegan. *Exploring American Healthcare through 50 Historic Treasures*. Lanham, MD: Rowman & Littlefield, 2021.

Klockars, Karl. *Beer Lover's Chicago: Best Breweries, Brewpubs and Beer Bars*. Guilford, CT: Globe Pequot, 2018.

Kogan, Rick. "Ale House Mainstay Puts Life on Page." *Chicago Tribune*, November 24, 2015.

———. "At News of the Death of a Bartender, Memories of O'Rourke's Pour Forth." *Chicago Tribune*, October 11, 2018.

———. *A Chicago Tavern: A Goat, a Curse, and the American Dream*. Chicago: Lake Claremont Press, 2006.

———. "Haunted by the Past: Landmark Harry Caray's Was a Mobster's Hideout, Has Secret Rooms and Sits on Chicago's Block No. 1." *Chicago Tribune*, August 30, 2020.

———. "The Tale of 'The Black Widow': In Gangster History of Chicago, Hidden in the Shadows Is Where One Can Find Annette Nitti." *Chicago Tribune*, September 1, 2020.

Laing, Olivia. *The Trip to Echo Spring: On Writers and Drinking*. New York: Picador, 2014.

Lait, Jack, and Lee Mortimer. *Chicago Confidential*. New York: Crown Publishers, 1950.

La Pointe, Michael. "The Black Gambling King of Chicago." *Paris Review*, April 7, 2020.

Lindberg, Richard. *Chicago by Gaslight: A History of Chicago's Netherworld 1880–1920*. Chicago: Academy Chicago Publishers, 1996.

———. *The Gambler King of Clark Street: Michael C. McDonald and the Rise of Chicago's Democratic Machine*. Carbondale: Southern Illinois University Press, 2017.

Lorenz, Alfred Lawrence. "The Whitechapel Club: Defining Chicago's Newspapermen in the 1890s." *American Journalism* 15, no. 1 (Winter 1998).

McClelland, Edward. "The Chicago Political Quote Hall of Fame." *Chicago*, January 13, 2020.

Metz, Nina. "The City That Drinks: Chicago Bar Culture on Film." *Chicago Tribune*, June 4, 2015.

Moehringer, J.R. *The Tender Bar: A Memoir*. New York: Hachette Books, 2015.

Moser, Whet. "The Decline of the Chicago Neighborhood Tavern: A Daley and Demographic Legacy." *Chicago Magazine*, February 13, 2012.

Nagrant, Michael. "Everyone Has a Favorite Chicago Dive Bar: This One's Mine." *Chicago Tribune*, March 24, 2017.

Neu, Denise. *Chicago by the Pint: A Craft Beer History of the Windy City*. Charleston, SC: The History Press, 2001.

Noel, Josh. "At Goose Island, a Swan Song for Its Honker's Ale." *Chicago Tribune*, March 13, 2019.

———. *Barrel-Aged Stout and Selling Out: Goose Island, Anheuser-Busch, and How Craft Beer Became Big Business*. Chicago: Chicago Review Press, 2018.

———. "Chicago's Decade of Beer: The Breweries That Shaped the City's Craft Scene." *Chicago Tribune*, January 8, 2020.

Bibliography

———. "Don't Sneer at This Beer Anymore: Not Just Dry January: Sales of Nonalcoholic Brew Are Growing." *Chicago Tribune*, January 24, 2021.

———. "Getting Crafty: Revolution Brewing Becomes Illinois' Top-Selling Craft Brewery, Besting Blue Moon and Goose Island." *Chicago Tribune*, March 10, 2020.

———. "Hopleaf, Map Room Turning 25." *Chicago Tribune*, March 29, 2017.

———. "Is the Pandemic Issuing Last Call?" *Chicago Tribune*, August 9, 2020.

———. "Looking Back at Goose Island Sale a Decade Later." *Chicago Tribune*, April 1, 2021.

———. "Tap Dancing: Four New Breweries Opening in Chicago Despite the Pandemic—Even If Some Owners Wish They Could Wait." *Chicago Tribune*, July 17, 2020.

Okrent, Daniel. *Last Call: The Rise and Fall of Prohibition*. New York: Scribner, 2010.

Oldenburg, Ray. *The Great Good Place: Cafés, Coffee Shops, Community Centers, Beauty Parlors, General Stores, Bars, Hangouts, and How They Get You through the Day*. New York: Paragon House, 1989.

Oliver, Garrett, ed. *The Oxford Companion to Beer*. Foreword by Tom Colicchio. New York: Oxford University Press, 2012.

Pacyga, Dominic. *American Warsaw: The Rise, Fall, and Rebirth of Polish Chicago*. Chicago: University of Chicago Press, 2019.

———. *Chicago: A Biography*. Chicago: University of Chicago Press, 2009.

Parnell, Sean. *Historic Bars of Chicago*. Chicago: Lake Claremont Press, 2010.

Porter, James. "Bernice Never Imagined She'd Be Running Bernice's Tavern." *Chicago Reader*, March 15, 2015.

Reardon, Patrick T. "Tapped Out." *Chicago Tribune Sunday Magazine*, June 13, 2004.

Renner, Richard Wilson. "In a Perfect Ferment: Chicago, the Know-Nothings, and the Riot for Lager Beer." *Chicago History* 5, no. 3 (Fall 1976).

Riley, Joshua. "Conrad Seipp Brews Again." *Chicago Reader*, March 22, 2021.

Samarov, Dmitry. *Old Style*. Chicago: Pictures & Blather, 2021.

Savage, Bill. "Can a Division Street Cocktail Bar Truly Capture the Spirit of Nelson Algren?" *Chicago Reader*, June 13, 2018.

Sawyers, June. "Atlas Obscura's First Ward Ball Celebrates Chicago's Bawdy Levee District History." *Third Coast Review*, January 29, 2019.

———. *Chicago Portraits*. Foreword by Rick Kogan. Evanston, IL: Northwestern University Press, 2012.

Bibliography

———. *Chicago Sketches: Urban Tales, Stories, and Legends from Chicago History*. Chicago: Wild Onion Books/Loyola Press, 1995.

Schnitzler, Nicole. "This Legendary Chicago Bartender Will Serve You Marriage and Financial Advice." *Vice*, July 21, 2017.

Seely, Mike. "Dive Bars Aren't Down for the Count." *New York Times*, November 12, 2020.

Selvam, Ashok. "38-Year Shinnick's Pub Bartender on Preserving Chicago's Neighborhood Tavern Culture." *Eater Chicago*, October 21, 2014.

Sisson, Patrick. "Getting to Know Rainbo Club through Its Regulars." *Eater Chicago*, October 1, 2012.

Skilnik, Bob. "Building Chicago Was Thirsty Work; Brewers Rolled in with a Solution." *Chicago Tribune*, July 16, 1997.

———. *The History of Brewing in Chicago: 1833–1978*. Fort Lee, NJ: Barricade Books, 2006.

Slingerland, Edward. *Drunk: How We Sipped, Danced, and Stumbled Our Way to Civilization*. New York: Little, Brown, 2021.

Smith, Jake. "A Tavern on (Almost) Every Corner: Why Did So Many Chicago Bars Disappear." April 6, 2019. www.wbez.org.

Sula, Mike. "Wanda's World." *Chicago Reader*, January 24, 2008.

Taubeneck, Anne. "Down to the Last Detail." *Chicago Tribune*, January 7, 2001.

Thiel, Julia. "Bars on Residential Streets Are Chicago's 'Great Good Places.'" *Chicago Reader*. www.chicagoreader.com.

Washburn, Charles. *Come into My Parlor: A Biography of the Notorious Everleigh Sisters of Chicago*. New York: Bridgehead, 1954.

Wendt, Lloyd, and Herman Kogan. *Lords of the Levee: The Story of Bathhouse John and Hinky Dink*. 1943. Repr., Foreword by Rick Kogan. Evanston, IL: Northwestern University Press, 2005.

Whiteis, David. "In Billy Branch's Blues, the Legendary Palm Tavern Still Stands." *Chicago Reader*, February 2, 2015.

Wong, Grace, and Patrick M. O'Connell. "At 136, Schaller's Pump Serves Its Final Round." *Chicago Tribune*, May 1, 2017.

Zywicki, Joseph B. "Chapin & Gore's 'Jolly Portrait Gallery.'" *Chicago History* 15, no. 3 (Fall 1986).

Bibliography

Websites that I found useful include:

Block Club
Chicago Bar Project
Chicago City Wire
Chicago Detours
Chicagology.com
Digital Research Library of Illinois History Journal, Neil Gale, PhD, DRLOIJjournal.blogspot.com
Eater Chicago
Gapers Block
Jazz Age Chicago
Lakeview Historical Chronicles
My Al Capone Museum
Mysteriouschicago.com
Old Breweries.com
Realbeer.com
Restaurant-ing through History
Rogerebert.com
Thrillist
Time Out Chicago

ABOUT THE AUTHOR

Born in Glasgow, Scotland, June Skinner Sawyers is the author of more than twenty-five books, including several books on Chicago. She was a regular contributor to *Chicago Tribune*, where she wrote three columns at various times: on local history, nightlife and travel books. She teaches at the Newberry Library in Chicago.